Short Study
OF THE
OLD
TESTAMENT

REV. DR. JACKSON YENN-BATAH

WESTBOW
PRESS®
A DIVISION OF THOMAS NELSON
& ZONDERVAN

WestBow Press books may be ordered through booksellers or by contacting:

WestBow Press
A Division of Thomas Nelson & Zondervan
1663 Liberty Drive
Bloomington, IN 47403
www.westbowpress.com
844-714-3454

Because of the dynamic nature of the Internet, any web addresses or links contained in this book may have changed since publication and may no longer be valid. The views expressed in this work are solely those of the author and do not necessarily reflect the views of the publisher, and the publisher hereby disclaims any responsibility for them.

Any people depicted in stock imagery provided by Getty Images are models, and such images are being used for illustrative purposes only. Certain stock imagery © Getty Images.

Scripture quotations are taken from The Holy Bible, New International Version®, NIV® Copyright © 1973, 1978, 1984, 2011 by Biblica, Inc.® Used by permission. All rights reserved worldwide.

ISBN: 978-1-6642-8047-2 (sc)
ISBN: 978-1-6642-8046-5 (e)

Print information available on the last page.

WestBow Press rev. date: 11/04/2022

D E D I C A T I O N

This book"Short Study of the Old Testament"
is dedicated to my beloved son
Andrew Yenn-Batah, Financial Consultant.
Your love, devotion and care inspires me daily
to higher service to the LORD.
Peace, love and grace abide with you always. Love you Drew.

PREFACE

"Short Study of the Old Testament" was written as a result of a weekly Bible Study with my Congregation at Wesley United Methodist Church in Arlington Texas to encourage them to read and study the Old Testament for guidance, comfort and strength in their daily Christian life.

Believing that the stories and people in the Old Testament serve as examples for believers today, my intent of writing this book is to give a short explanation of the main gist of each of the 39 books of the Old Testament to help the reader to have a fair understanding of each book and to start reading the Old Testament with new interest and excitement.

By reading the Old Testament, I hope readers will understand the New Testament better because all the teachings and events in the Old Testament give us the background to all that happened when Jesus was born and during his life.

For example, understanding the Old Testament' sacrifices shed light on what Jesus' sacrifice on the Cross means.

It is my hope that readers will enjoy this Short Study of the Old Testament and therefore become better Christians through obedience to the LORD.

My sincere thanks and gratitude to all my Bible Study students at Wesley United Methodist Church, the Church leaders and my devoted ministerial staff Rev Kate Thompson and Mrs Eno Afon (Candidate for Ordained Ministry) for their support, commitment and service to the Lord at Wesley United Methodist Church, Arlington Texas.

Grace, peace, love and God's blessings to you all.

JYB.

CONTENTS

CHAPTER 1

The Origin of the Bible

At the beginning of our "Short Study of the Old Testament", we need to know a few things about the Bible first. The Bible makes it clear that God inspired the whole Bible in 2 Timothy 3:16-17. " All scripture is God inspired and is useful for teaching, rebuking, correcting and training in righteousness, So that the man of God may be thoroughly equipped for every good work".

The Bible is made up of 66 books that were written over a period of 1,000 years by more than forty individuals inspired by God. In the Old Testament, we have 39 books and in the New Testament 27 books.

The Old Testament was written in Hebrew with some Aramaic while the New Testament was written in Koine Greek - a dialect of ancient Greek that merchants and travelers used. Before the printing press was invented, around 1440 AD in Germany, the Bible was copied by hand by special scribes who developed intricate methods of counting words and letters to ensure that no errors are made. The Bible was the first book ever printed on the printing press by Gutenberg Press i1455– the Latin Bible. Today, there is much evidence that the Bible we have is remarkably true to the original writings of the many copies made by hand before the year 1500AD. More than 5,900 Greek manuscripts from the New Testament alone still exists today. The text of the Bible is better preserved than any other writings in the world.

Amanzingly, the discovery of the Dead Sea Scrolls, in 1946-1947 at the Qumran Caves, confirm the astonishing reliability of some of the copies of the Old Testament made over the years. Although some spelling variation exist, no variation has affected basic Bible doctrine. As the Bible was carried to the other countries over the years, it has been translated into the common languages of the people by scholars who wanted others to know God's word.

If you are wondering why or what is the reason for studying the Bible, here are some simple reasons:

Studying the Bible enables us to know God. God created heaven and earth and everyone in it (Genesis Chapter 1-3) and to know God is to have eternal life (John 17:3).

Studying the Bible enables us to enjoy and love God by meditating on God's character, principles, and promises. In doing so, we rejoice in his love, care, and forgiveness (Psalm 119:12-18, 1 Timothy 6:17).

We learn to understand God's word, to learn direction in life, to find comfort and hope, to become pure and holy, and to "Obey His Great Commandment" which is to love God with all of our being and our neighbor as ourselves (Mark 12:29-31), and Jesus' commandment to love one another (John 13:34-35).

Exploring the Old Testament, therefore, provides us with the background of each book so we can become acquainted with the lands and cultures in the Bible. This allows us to travel through the book so we can enjoy the richness and beauty of the scriptures. Additionally, there are major themes in each biblical book to help us grasp the main message of each book.

Finally, we discover that Jesus is the center and star of God's revelation as shown in each book to guide us understand God's plan of salvation and restoration.

What is the Old Testament?

The Old Testament is the Word of God as much as the New Testament. It was complied over hundreds of years and written by many different authors; it all originated with God. It is God's word to his people. The Apostle Peter explains to believers that we also have the prophetic message as something completely reliable--- "No prophecy of scripture came about by the Prophets' own interpretation of things. For prophecy never had its origin in the human will, but prophets, through human, spoke from God as they were carried along by the Holy Spirit (2 Peter 1:19-21).

    The Old Testament helps us to understand the New Testament. It deals with events and teachings hundreds of years before Jesus Christ was born. These events and teachings give us the background to all that happened when Jesus was born and during his life. This means understanding the Old Testament's sacrifices shed light on what Jesus' sacrificed on the cross means. It helps us to know about the Old Testament prophecies of a coming Messiah (the Christ) who will fulfill God's promises given long ago. Also, the Old Testament laws, customs, and religious traditions help us to make sense of Jesus' interactions with the Jewish religious leaders of his day. Above all, the Old Testament helps us to see God's grace for humanity. We see and begin to understand the gracious and powerful God who created all things, we see God's grace as we contemplate human sin and folly. We see his grace: rather than destroying, we see God's plan to save us. This unfolds in the pages of the Old Testament as we read through. Our eyes are opened as we see God's plan in the stories of people who experienced the goodness of creation, the corruption of a good creation, the terrible disturbing power of sin, and the sad consequences of our separation from God.

The Old Testament and the stories we read, serve as examples for all believers today. We are reminded by Paul that things that happened to God's people in the Old Testament, happened to them as example and were written down as warnings for us. So if we think we are standing firm, we must be careful that we don't fal. (1 Corinthians 10:11-12).

We see in the Old Testament that even most faithful people like Moses and King David, fell into sin and were disciplined by God. Yet we see in the Old Testament how God continued to redeem and restore his people even after terrible sin and tragedy. Today, all believers have been sent by Jesus to be witnesses of his love, grace, and sacrifice. As long as we are in the world, we must learn to recognize the way God moves and acts in the world, through people, and sometimes in extraordinary ways that do not require people. The more we read the Old Testament, the more we learn and recognize God's ways in the world. The Old Testament is divided into sections. The following are the books in the Old Testament:

SECTION 1 THE TORAH/ PENTATEUCH	SECTION 2 THE HISTORICAL BOOKS
Genesis Exodus Leviticuis Numbers Deuteronomy	Joshua Judges Ruth 1&2 Samuel 1&2 Kings 1&2 Chronicles Ezra & Nehemial Esther

SECTION 3. POETRY AND WISDOM.	SECTION 4 THE PROPHETIC BOOKS		
Job Psalms Proverbs Ecclesiastes Song of Songs	**Major Prophets**	**Minor Prophets**	
	Isaiah Jeremiah Lamentation Ezekiel Daniel	Hosea Joel Amos Obadiah Jonah Micah	Nahum Habakkuk Zephaniah Haggai Zechariah Malachi

Our journey through the Old Testament starts with section 1, the Torah (Hebrew) or the Pentateuch (Greek). In the Old Testament, the Torah or Pentateuch refers to the first five books of the Bible. The word "Pentateuch" comes from a Greek word that means "five vessels or scrolls", In Hebrew, this section is known as the Torah- the law or instruction. On a deeper level, the Pentateuch is God's gracious provision for his people. It provides an identity for God's people, provides the answers to the questions. "What does it mean to be God's people and how can we be God's people?" The Pentateuch, therefore is God's instructions for a nation learning to be God's people while living in the world. For this reason, the Pentateuch lays the basis for the rest of the Bible. It explains the origin of the universe, of nations, and of God's people. It explains the need for God's direct intervention in human history and human sin. It shows how God acts in the lives of his people. In light of this, the main characters in the Pentateuch are God, Abraham, Israel, Moses and the promised land. Now, let us get started on our short journey through the Old Testament. Enjoy the exploration.

CHAPTER 3

Genesis: The Beginning Story

———

The Book of Genesis is about beginnings. It tells us the beginning of all things, the nations, God's people, Israel. It spans many hundreds of years than any other book of the Bible. The years include the very beginning of the universe to the time when Abraham's descendants fled to Egypt to escape a famine around 1800 BC.

Genesis tells us about the good beginning of creation, the beginning of all human problems and the beginning of God's solution to those problems. Chapter 1-2, tells about the origin of the world Chapter 2-4 tells about the origin of nations. Chapter 11-26 tells about the origin of Israel.

The <u>Origin of the World</u> centers on the theme of creation, sovereignty, Humans as God's image and human responsiblitiy. All these themes involved God and human beings.

The <u>Origin of Nations</u> focuses on the theme human failure and sin, death, sin and punishment, promise and grace.

The <u>Origin of Israel</u> covers the theme covenant, God's plans of redemption, God's people, God's work through family and God's work through the nations.

In the <u>Origin of Nations</u>, the people involved are Adam and Eve, the Serpent, Cain and Abel, Noah, Abraham and Sarah Hagar, Lot, Isaac and Rebekcah, Jacob, Leah, Bilhah, Zilpah Jacobs 12 sons, Tamar and Potiphar. As we read through the Book of Genesis, there are major things that we see. We see that God is the creator of all things, the world, the nations, and Israel. The amazing thing we see is that creation is the beginning of relationships. God wants to relate to his creation, especially to humans.

But the problem is that although God created all things and was pleased with them, humans abused their freedom and because of sin, they broke their relationship with God, with each other and with nature. We also see that instead of God leaving them in their rebellion and corruption, God extended his grace to humanity. He promised to act directly to solve the human problem by announcing the coming of one who would crash the head of the deceiving serpent (Genesis 3:15). Many years later, on the cross, Jesus crushed Satan's head.

To fulfill God's plan of restoration, God chose the family of Abraham to start over. God made a covenant with Abraham. He relates, guides, rescues, and provides for the family he has chosen. The author of the Book of Genesis is not named, but Jewish and Christian tradition have accepted that the author of Genesis and the other four books of the Torah/ Pentateuch were written by Moses between 1446 BC and 1406 BC the possible date of Moses death.

Reading through the Book of Genesis, one finds that in Chapter 12, we are introduced to Abraham. God calls him to leave his hometown in Ur to travel to the land of Caanan, the Promised Land. It was a business center in the second millennium (2000) BC, and was located in Southern Iraq. Archaelogical remains attest to the glory and importance of the city.

Canaan, the land that God instructed Abraham to travel to, was surrounded by powerful kingdoms: the Mesopotamian Kingdoms of Assyria and Babylonia to the north, and Egypt to the South. In Genesis 11:31-12:7, we see God tell Abram to go to Caanan. Abram travels from his hometown Ur in the summer to Caanan, the Promised Land. And God promises to give the land to Abram's descendants.

The Book of Genesis ends with Abraham's descendants no longer living in Caanan, but in Northern Egypt in the land of Goshen. So what we learn in the Book of Genesis is that God reveals himself as the creator and king, who loves his creation. He plans to redeem humanity through a person and family, so all nations and creation itself, will be blessed. God chose Abraham and his descendants to be blessed and to be a blessing to others. Even though each person like Isaac, Judah and even Joseph, had shortcomings, God still used them to fulfill his promises.

Today, God is on a mission to redeem his creation. As he called people in ancient times to be part of that mission, he continues to call believers today. Abraham by faith, when called to go to a place he would later receive as his inheritance, obeyed and went eventhough he did not know where he was going, it took faith. Just as in the Old Testament times, it still takes faith for us today to let God lead us to where he wants us to go, especially when we do not know what lies ahead.

CHAPTER 4

Exodus: From Slavery to a Nation

The Book of Exodus is a story about God saving his people from slavery and forming them into a nation. While Genesis tells us about the beginning of all things, the Book of Exodus tells us more on the origin of God's people. God gives Moses the law which is more than a series of rules of behavior. God's instruction to Israel, shaped the nation and gave boundaries for the safety of the people. The law showed the people of Israel what it meant to be God's people in the midst of other nations.

In addition, Exodus connects creation with redemption. We see this in the redeeming or liberation of Israel from Egypt and God creating new people, his people. It must be observed that the first five books of the Bible called the Pentateuch in Greek and Torah in Hebrew, has the purpose of instructing Israel on what it means to be God's people in the midst of other nations. So as we read through these books, we must be aware of God's expectation from the people of Israel.

The setting of the book is in Egypt. At the beginning, we see Israel enslaved in Egypt and God calls Moses from the burning bush to go deliver God's people from slavery in Egypt. Moses goes and confronts Pharaoh the king of Egypt to set the Israelites free but Pharaoh would not let them go. So God sends ten plagues upon Egypt and the first passover was instituted, followed by the Exodus and the parting of the Red Sea (Chapters 1:1-15:2). In chapters 15:22-18:27, we see Israel on the way to Sinai; God traveling with them in the wilderness, God provides manna, quail, and water from a rock to feed and preserve them. Then at Sinai, God instructs and organizes his people in (Chapter 19:1-40:38). It is at Mount Sinai that Moses meets with God and receives the Ten Commandments for the people of Israel. It was during this time that Moses received instructions for the tabernacle. Unfortunately, one bad behavior of the people of Israel is that while Moses was away receiving the Ten Commandments, they turned away from worshiping God to worship the golden calf. When Moses returned to see the sight of the people worshiping the golden calf, he became angry and threw down the two tables, breaking them. He burnt the golden calf in a fire to the ground which turned into powder, scattered it on water, and forced the Israelites to drink it to teach them a lesson.

The stories in Exodus are very interesting and eye-opening to all who profess to be believers: God is a redeemer and rescuer. He is the supreme God, and he has control over his creation. Not only that but also the stories teach us that God is a provider. Above all, the stories teach us that God is king, God is just and merciful, God is with his people, and God's desire is to relate personally to his people. We can attest to this in Chapters 1:1-15:21, 15:22-18:27 and 19:1-40:38. When we study the book of Exodus carefully, we will note fifteen points about God and the people of Israel.

- Egypt oppressed Israel and became God's enemy.
- God heard their cry and remembered his commitment to Abraham.
- Moses, a child of slaves, was threatened to be killed along with many other children. However, God rescued him. God called and sent Moses to free his people from Egypt.
- The Exodus: God through Moses, confronted Pharaoh in a struggle for the future of Israel. After ten terrible plagues, Pharoah relented and freed Israel.

- The day of redemption was celebrated and commemorated in the feast of the Passover.
- God saved Israel from Pharaoh's army through one more spectacular miracle by parting the Red Sea.

In all these, God shows us that he is our redeemer and rescuer, He is the supreme king, and has control over his creation.

The other points are:

- God led Israel through the wilderness of Zin toward his holy mountain at Sinai.
- He provided for the people's needs during the journey in the wilderness.
- We see Israel grumble against Moses and God.
- God brought Israel to meet with him at Sinai.

These points show us that God is our provider. Lastly, the following points show us that God is king, just and merciful, God is with his people and he wants to relate personally to his people.

- On Mount Sinai, God instructed Moses on God's law for Israel. These laws teach Israel how to become God's holy nation.
- The people grew restless at Moses's delay on the mountain. They built for themselves a golden calf to worship. God punished them. However because Moses interceded for them, God did not destroy them.
- God ordered Moses to build a special dwelling, the tabernacle. God's presence would travel with the people to the place he promised Abraham, Issac and Jacob.
- God equipped the Israelites to carry on the building of the tabernacle.
- Once the tabernacle was completed, God's presence descended to dwell in it.

As we read through the Book of Exodus, we will come across people such as Moses, Aaron, Pharoah and Miriam who all played major roles in Exodus. Lastly, we find the command: " I am the Lord your God, who brought you out of Egypt, out of slavery. You shall not have other gods before me" (Exodus 20:2-3). May this remind us as Christians to be faithful to our God in our life's journey.

C H A P T E R   5

Leviticus: Forming a Worshipping Nation

The Book of Leviticus forms the heart of the Torah (Hebrew) and the Pentateuch (Greek). In Hebrew, the Torah which is often translated as "law" is better translated as "instruction". In the Bible, therefore, the Torah refers to the ten Commandments, the law of Moses or the five Books of Moses: Genesis, Exodus, Leviticus, Numbers and Deuteronomy.

One main function of the first five books of the Bible is to give an identity to God's people. And the core of this identity is the Book of Leviticus which centers on holiness. The book is not full of dry and boring rules, but it is a wellspring of holiness - the living God, the God of Abraham, Issac and Jacob, the God who defeated Egypt and divided the waters and the God whose presence dwells in the tabernacle. Leviticus teaches the people of Israel how to live safely in the presence of this Holy God. Reading the book may be boring with rules and regulations yet it is a wonderful spiritual exercise to undertake to acquaint ourselves with the Holy God of Israel. The themes of the book are: Sacrifice and God's Grace; Priests, Purity, the Day of Atonement and Holy Living.

A. Sacrifices were God's merciful provision for Israel in order for the people to dwell with a Holy God. Even though sacrifices are not necessary today because Jesus' sacrifice on the Cross was sufficient, Leviticus helps us to understand the meaning and importance of Jesus' sacrifice. In the Old Testament, the shedding of blood and the use of animal blood for purifying and atoning rituals, was a reminder for the worshiper that a life had been taken and that the cost of sin is high indeed. Therefore, the sacrifice of an animal for atonement of sins, allowed the Israelites to dwell alongside God as his presence dwell in the tabernacle.

Chapters 1-7 of Leviticus give instructions about sacrifices: burnt offering, grain offering, fellowship offering, sin offering and guilt offering.

B. The Priests were intermediaries. At different times and in different ways during their ministries, priests stood in the gap that separates God and humans. Their holiness did not come from their actions or position. Rather, their holiness depended on their nearness to the tabernacle, to God's presence. As such, they were held to rigorous moral, ritual and purity standards. In Leviticus, the instructions about priests are recorded in Chapters 8-10 covering Aaron and his sons and how the priests present offerings.

C. The Day of Atonement was a feast that climax the liturgical calendar. On the Day of Atonement, the high priest made atonement for sin in the tabernacle. It was God's way to bring reconciliation and restoration to the problem of human sin and its effect. The process was this: the high priest would take two animals, pray on one, lay the guilt of the whole nation on it, and send it out of the camp into the desert. Then he would sacrifice the second animal and bring its blood into the most holy place in the tabernacle to offer it to God. By God's grace, we are fortunate today because by Christ's sacrifice on the cross he bore our guilt and fully paid the price for human sin. We therefore, do not need any other sacrifice for our sins.

Leviticus Chapter 16 gives instructions on the Day of Atonement.

D. <u>Ritual Purity</u> lays emphasis on the fact that purity was necessary as people lived around the tabernacle. God's presence rejects the ritually impure. Purification rites were therefore God's provision for the people to be able to approach God's presence. Thank God, instead of ritual purity, today we are called to godliness in 2 Peter 1:3-8. Instructions about ritual purity is recorded in Leviticus Chapter 11-15 covering clean and unclean foods and the purity laws.

E. <u>Holy Living</u> is not a life filled with dread and mired in guilt. It is rather a hopeful, joyful, and satisfied way of living. It is life lived according to God's original plans. The many rules, laws, and ordinances in the Bible are boundaries that guide us during our lives. Although many regulations depend on sacrificial purity rituals, they have become redundant today after Christ's sacrifice on the cross. However the principles on which they operated continue to be relevant for us today. Whereas the Israelites could see the presence of God in the tabernacle, we experience it in a more direct way because God's presence, the Holy Spirit, dwells in us. "Do you not know that you are a temple of God and that the Spirit of God dwells in you?" (1 Corinthians 3:16).

In Leviticus, instructions for holy living are given in Chapters 17-27. They cover animal sacrifices, sexual relations, punishment for sins, priestly requirements, the sabbath, feasts, the year of Jubilee and above all, God's favor and the consequences of disobedience. As we read through the book, we must remember that the focus is on equipping God's people to become God's holy nation of Israel and that the heart of the Torah is holiness. Take time to enjoy reading the Book of Levitiucus.

CHAPTER 6

Numbers: The Old Yeild for the New

The Book of Numbers is a story about the rebellion and disobedience of Israel. Yet it is also a story of grace and mercy. The book narrates the years God's people, Israel spent traveling in the wilderness, depicting them as God's army advancing toward the promised land. In the book, we see that even when the people grumbled and rebelled, God's grace availed. Because God is also God of justice, the people were still punished for their rebellion, but God did not destroy them. Rather, God extended his grace to the coming generation.

In the book, we see two generations. We see the end of the old generation that came out of Egypt and a new generation under Joshua. The old generation spans Chapters 1-25 and the new generation spans Chapters 26-36. In chapters 1-25, the first census is taken, regulations for purity and offering are instituted, the Israelites leave Sinai and grumble, twelve spies explore Canaan, the people rebel, God instructs Moses and Aaron and lastly, the Israelites face challenges: thirst, venomous snakes, and hostile nations. In Chapters 26-36, the second census is taken, Joshua is commissioned to succeed Moses, the laws for offerings, feasts and vows are instituted, the Israelites defeat their enemies, and the new generation receive instructions for when they enter the Promised Land.

There are two words that need explanation here: "The wilderness" and "The Census". In Numbers, the word "wilderness" is very important. In addition to the literal meaning of the Israelites crossing the wilderness to get to the promise land, the concept of wilderness had a symbolic meaning as well. The wilderness was a place of danger, of death and barreness, of chaos and darkness. It represented a life- giving will. The wilderness, therefore became a symbol of God's absence and of evil itself.

On the other hand, the wilderness came to represent a place of transition, a place for meeting God. The tabernacle and its surroundings in the wilderness with God's presence, became a place of life, hope, order and light. As we understand this definition of the wilderness, we will understand and appreciate the Book of Numbers and the events it unfolds. Now to the word "Census". There were two census taken in the Book of Numbers. The census numbers reported that there was a fighting force of six hundred thousand (600,000), which suggest that the population at this time was more than two million. So such a large population wandering in the wilderness for forty years, would require a miracle to be supported and survive. And that is exactly what we see happened. God miraculously provided for the Israelites through their journey. A lesson to us that God provides for his people.

In the Book of Exodus, God promised the Israelites that he would be with them on their way to the Promised Land (Exodus 33:14). In Numbers, we see that despite Israel's unfaithfulness, and hardness of heart, God remained to his promise. His presence remained with Israel, and his protection and provision follow them through the wilderness (Numbers11:21-23, 31-32). Even in the middle of the wilderness, when everything seemed disarray, dark, and hopeless, God's grace continued to offer new hope for the future. If there is any lesson we can learn from the Book of Numbers, it is that traveling through this wilderness of life can often be a grueling test to our faith, and it is all too natural to respond with anger. But journing through these difficulties should remind us to depend on God and trust that he will be faithful to his promises to us. Our God is merciful, gracious and faithful. From generation to generation his faithfulness never ends.

Deuteronomy: A Time Between

The Book of Deuteronomy is the last of the Torah. It describes the people of Israel in a time in between. Finally, after spending forty years in the wilderness, they arrived at the promised land but had not entered it yet.. In Deuteronomy, Moses repeated God's instructions for the second generation of God's people. It consists of mostly the speeches that Moses gave to the second generation on the plains of Moab before they entered the Promised Land. The first generation who left Egypt and witnessed God's mighty acts of salvation had died - except Joshua, Caleb and Moses. The second generation had not witnessed first hand the powerful acts of God against Egypt nor his awesome glory revealed on Mount Sinai. Moses therefore took long pause to instruct this new generation what makes them God's people and challenges them to find their identity and purpose in the covenant with God.

As they waited at the edge of the Promised Land, God's promises were already there to the reaching hand but not yet fulfilled. The focus points of the Book of Deuteronomy are: God's instruction for a new generation, God's instructions for a generation at the entrance of the Promised Land and basing the identity of God's people on the covenant. A reminder of the Old Testament Covenants is helpful here.

In Genesis 9:8-17, we have the Noah covenant. God promised not to destroy again his creation.

- In Genesis 15:19-21, we have the Abraham covenant. God promised to give Abraham's descendants the land. The covenant was sealed with an animal sacrifice.
- In Genesis 17, another Abraham covenant. God confirmed his covenant with Abraham and made a commitment and reaffirmed his promise of land and Abraham agreed to keep the sign of the covenant: circumcision.
- In Exodus 19-24, we have the covenant at Sanai. God promised to make Israel his people and also expressed what he expected of Israel.
- In Numbers 25:10-31, Phinehas covenant. God granted Phinehas, a priest, a descendant of Aaron and his descendants a "covenant of lasting priest hood" (25:13).
- In 2 Samuel 7:5-16, we have the Davidic covenant. God promised to preserve David's descendants on the throne of Israel.
- Lastly in Jeremiah 31:31-34, we have the new covenant. God declared that "he will make a new covenant with the people of Israel and with the people of Judah" (31:31). This new covenant establishes a new relationship with his people by writing his law on their hearts.

Understanding those covenants, help us to understand and appreciate the faithfulness of God. The Book of Deuteronomy is divided into five sections. Section 1 looks back and summarizes the wilderness wanderings (Chapters 1-3). Section 2 deals with the Great discourse (4-11). It stresses on fear, love, and obey God. It also emphasizes the Ten Commandments. The covenant stipulations (12-16), highlights the worship of one true God in one place and various laws for Israel. The covenant ceremony is in Chapters 27-30. It is about the blessings and curses of the covenant. And lastly, a look forward in Chapter 31-34, Joshua is confirmed as Moses successor, the song and blessings of Moses, and Moses death on Mount Nebo. The Book of Deuteronomy, is a reminder to God's people that God is faithful to his covenant. He is the Holy God, full of mercy and grace, who led his people to the Promised Land. The next generation is challenged to remember and learn from the mistakes of the previous generation (1 Corinthians 10:1-13).

In Deuteronomy, the second generation is reminded to not forget the source of their blessings, not take the land for granted, nor become like the people living in the land, not make idols for themselves, nor rely on their economic or politics power to survive or abandon the covenant. We too stand at the borders of the promised land - the New Jerusalem. We are already enjoying but some of God's wonderful promise is yet to be fulfilled. As the Israelites required instuctions to live in the land of God, we are also learning to live in the presence of God today. This closes our overview of the torah and we shall in the next chapter, overview the Historical Books of the Old Testament.

CHAPTER 8

Introduction to the Historical Books

The Historical Books form the second section of the Bible. This section continues from where section one ended. At the end of section one, Torah / Pentetauch, the Israelites are at the edge of the promised land after hearing instructions, advice and commands from Moses. When Moses died on Mount Nebo (Deuteronomy 34:1-12), God chose Joshua, Moses's longtime assistant, to lead the Israelites into the land. Now this section deals with Israel's historical experience with the land and God. These books range from conquering, settling, and experiencing the many joys, temptations, failures, and challenges of living in a land as the Israelites learned how to live as God's people. The Books cover a period of the history of Israel from the time of the conquest around 1400 BC to the time of Ezra and Nehemiah around 400 BC. In between, we find a dramatic history of the people, their kings, many painful disappointments, and some remarkable achievements. The people of Israel changed from a loosely organized group of twelve tribes to a united kingdom under David and Solomon, and then a divided kingdom: Israel in the north with 19 kings who did evil in the eyes of God, and Judah in the south with 19 kings also, although eight did what is right in God's eyes. The dominant person in the Historical Books is king David. He and his descendants were chosen by God. And God would rule and bless his people through the house of David. From this promise, in time the Messianic hope would arise. The hope refers to God's people longing to be reformed and redeemed. In short, the Historical Books give us a theological account of Israel's failure to keep the covenant and God's compassionate and just dealings with them. The importance of the historical books cannot be overemphasized. They illustrate for us how God relates in history to his people and the whole world. The stories show us how God's will works out in history:

God works in direct ways, as in the stories of Joshua entering the promise land.

God works in indirect ways, as through prophets like Samuel and Elijah, or through other nations like Assyria or Babylon.

God works behind the scenesm as in the story of Esther,

If you are wondering what the Historical Books are, below is the list.

- Joshua
- Judges
- Ruth
- 1&2 Samuel
- 1&2 Kings
- 1&2 Chronicles
- Ezra & Nehemiah
- Esther

In the Historical Books there are very important events that we came a cross in the history of Israel. They include the calling of Abraham, the Exodus, entering the Promised Land, God's covenant with David and the building of the temple in Jerusalem. Two other important events were the Assyrian exile of the Northern Kingdom of Israel in 722 BC and the Babylonian exile of the Southern Kingdom of Judah (Jerusalem) in 586 BC. The Assyrians and Babylonians deported people they conquered from the newly conquered territories as a policy. The idea was to remove the possibility of rebellion and making it easy to control the territory. They did not relocate the entire population but rather, took to exile the nobles - kings, princes and princesses, priests and royal officers. They also moved other people from city to city and would finally destroy the capital cities of the kingdoms they conquered.

Exactly, that is what they did to Samaria in the Northern Kingdom and Jerusalem in Judah in the Southern Kingdom.q They made these cities almost inhabitable places. The Historical Books, along with the prophetic books, show that these were punishment for Israel and Judah's disloyalty to God. However, punishment is never God's final word. God restored the remnant of his people from Babylon. Ezra the priest and Nehemiah the governor returned with them to reorganize the religious and political life of the people in Jerusalem. By this, God was paving the way for the coming Messiah, the only one who could rescue humans from sin and death.

C H A P T E R   9

Joshua: Claiming the Promised Land.

The first book of the Historical Books is the Book of Joshua. In the Book of Deuteronomy, God's people Israel are prepared for the task ahead in the Promised Land and the Book of Joshua shows how God brought his people into the land and gave them rest. Joshua functions as a bridge between the wilderness experience and the time in the Promised Land. The book is named after Joshua whom God choose to be Moses' assistant since their journey from Egypt to Sinai (Exodus 17) and to become the leader of Israel after Moses' death (Deuteronomy 31). Briefly, the Book 1 of Joshua shows how and why Israel would eventually end up in exile. We are reminded in the book that sin and rebellion that would result in Israel's exile, began long before God executed his judgement against Israel and Judah. As we read through the book, we come across four parts of the book: the entrance where Joshua succeeds Moses, Rahab hides the spies, and the Israelites cross the Jordan River (Chapter 1-5). Conquest where we see the fall of Jericho, Achan's sin in the camp and it's consequences, and the battle against the kings and inhabitants in Chapter 5-12. The distribution of the land takes place in Chapters 13-21 and lastly the future in Chapters 22-24, covers Joshua's farewell and death. The setting of the book is very interesting. When

the Isralites came to the borders of the Promised Land, the political and military powerhouses of the area, Egypt and Mesopotania, were in a time of transition. The Canaanite kingdoms in the area were also independent and small. They were without an internal organization such as a government. This made it easier for the conquest to succeed. After the conquest, the land was divided among the twelve tribes: Reuben, Simeon, Zebulun, Judah, Dan, Naphtali, Gad, Asher, Issachar, Manasseh, Ephrain and Benjamin. The major themes of the book are:
God's faithfulness to his promises

- Conquest, settlement, and life in the land
- The covenant between God and Israel
- God's holiness and Judgement
- The unity of the people, and the role of Joshua as leader of Israel.

Some of the major characters we come across are Joshua whom God chose to be Israel's leader after the death of Moses. He organized, led and settled Israel in the land God had promised them. There was this woman called Rahab, she was a pagan prostitute who showed hospitality to Israel's spies, demonstrated an amazing faith in God, and became part of God's covenant people. She is listed as one of Jesus's ancestors in his genealogy recorded in Mathew 1:15. Achan is another major character. His disobedience caused Israel to loose an important battle against Ai. He took plunder from the battlefield when Israel had been instructed not to take anything. As a result of the lost of the battle, he was stoned to death as punishment (Joshua 7).

Two more people need highlighting: "Eleazor" and "Phinehas". Eleazor was the son of Aaron. He took over the high priests duties after Aaron died in Exodus 6:23 and Numbers 20:28. He helped Joshua to lead Israel into the Promised Land. Phinehas was the son of Eleazor the high priest and priest of Israel. His intervention to prevent the Israelites from polluting themselves and his zeal for God's covenant granted him a special covenant with God. He and his descendants would be priest of Israel forever (Joshua 22:13, 32-34 and 24:33).

Reading through the Book of Joshua, the shocking thing we come across is the conquest. It is shocking to come across the commands to

Israel to kill all inhabitants of the land, including women and children. But the answer is that God is serious about sin and it's consequences. In this case, God was using the Israelites as a tool to punish sin in the land. But as we find out in the Book of Judges, not all Canaanites were killed, since we find many of them living in the land after the conquest. The lesson we learn from the Book of Joshua is that God was faithful to his promises by giving his people victory and rest in the land. Also, God will prevail against his enemies because the whole universe belongs to him and he expects us to be courageous, obedient and trusting. I pray that we will take notes of this and seek the power of the Holy Spirit to make us faithful to our God. May the Book of Joshua, inspire us to obey the Lord always.

C H A P T E R   1 0

Judges: The Conflict
of Sin and Grace.

———

The Book of Judges is the seventh book of the Old Testament. The narrative in Judges covers the time between the conquest described in the Book of Joshua and the establishment of a kingdom in the Books of Samuel, during which biblical Judges served as temporary leaders. It is a narrative warning to all God's children against forgetting God's instruction and acting like the nations of the land. After the tribes of Israel settled in the promised land, they began a fast moral and spiritual decline. The problem was that there were still Canaanites left to fight because the conquest was incomplete. The Israelites were disobedient despite their claims to be faithful to God (Joshua 24:16-18). But even in those times when the Israelites turned their back to God, he was filled with compassion and mercy for them. He raised leaders known as Judges to deliver his people from oppression. The book offers a prophetic look at the history of God's people and contrasts God's faithfulness to humanties unfaithfulness and fickleness. One of its main purpose is to demonstrate the need for kings who would care for Israel's safety, lead the people to obedience of the law, and promote the pure worship of the Lord. The setting of the book is uncertain and the writer of the book is not known although some scholars think it was the Prophet Samuel who wrote it. The events the book describes occurred between the time of Joshua around 1400 BC and Samuel around 1000 BC in the Promised Land where the twelve tribes of Israel had settled.

In the book, we find that the Israelites were caught up in what is called the "Cycle Pattern of Judges." In the cycle, Israel disobeys God then they are oppressed by their enemies, Israel cries to God for deliverance, God raises up a deliver of judge to deliver them. Israel is delivered, Israel is at peace only to disobey God and fall back into the same cycle. In Chapter (1:1-3:6) we read about the incomplete conquest and the failing faith of Isarel. The cycle of sin and punishment is recorded in Chapters 3:7-16:31. The rest of the chapters are the mention of the various judges that God raised to deliver Isarel. The concluding chapters of 17-21 focuses on the spiritual and moral decay of the people of Israel.

The following is a list of the judges:

1. Othniel- 3:7-11, was from Judah and the Israelites were oppressed by the Mesopotamias for 8 years, Othniel delivered the Israelites from the Mesopotamias and they enjoyed peace for 40 years.

2. Ehud- 3:12-30, was from the tribe of Benjamin. He also fought and delivered the Israelites from the Mesopotamias who oppressed them for another 18 years after they had sin against God. This time they enjoyed a period of rest for 80 years before being oppressed again.

3. Shamgar- 3:31, was from unknown tribe. During his time, the Philistines were the oppressors. For how long, we do not know. But after Shamgar delivered the Israelites, they enjoyed peace for unknown period.

4. Deborah- Chapters 4-5, was of the tribe of Ephraim. The Canaanites rose against the Israelites and oppressed them for 20 years. It was Deborah who delivered them from the Canaanites and enjoy a period of peace for 40 years.

5. Gideon- Chapters 6-8, was from the tribe of Manasseh. The Midianites were the oppressors for 7 years and when Gideon delivered them, they enjoyed peace for 40 years.

6. <u>Tola</u>- Chapter 10:1-2, was from the tribe of Issacher. The oppressors were not known and the period of oppression is not known, but after they were delivered, Israel enjoy peace for 23 years before falling back into the cycle of sin.

7. <u>Jair</u>- Chapter 10:6-12:7, was from the tribes of Gilead- Manasseh. The oppressors are not mentioned and the period of oppression not known. But after the delivery, Israel enjoyed peace for Twenty-two years.

8. <u>Jephthah</u>- Chapter 10:16-12:7, was of the tribe of Gilead-Manasseh. During his time, the Ammorites were the oppressors of Israel. The period of oppressors we do not know but Israel enjoyed peace for 24 years after their deliverance.

9. <u>Ibzam</u>- Chapter 12:8-10, was of the tribe of Judah or Zebulun (not sure) and the oppressors are not known and the period is not known however, Israel enjoyed 7 years peace after their deliverance.

10. <u>Elon</u>- Chapter 12:11-12, was from the tribe of Zebulunin. Period of oppression and oppressors are not known but Israel enjoyed peace for 10 years under Elon.

11. <u>Abdon</u>- Chapter 12:13-15, was from tribe of Ephraim and delivered the Israelites from their enemies which are not mentioned. They enjoyed peace for 8 years.

12. <u>Samson</u>- Chapters 13-16, was from the tribe of Dan. The oppressors were the Philistines and they oppressed Israel for 40 years and when Samson delivered them they enjoyed peace for 20 years.

Of all those Judges,we are very familiar with the stories of Deborah, Gideon, and Samson but not very much about the others. Yet, they are the people that God used to show his mercy to the people of Israel in the midst of their struggle between sin and the grace of God.

In the book of Judges, therefore, we see themes of sin and punishment, God's justice and mercy, covenant loyalty and disloyalty, God's holiness and judgement and finaly the unity of God's people. Throughout Judges, God challenges the Israelites to be faithful to his covenant but they would not listen. Their rejection of God's instructions resulted in oppression and sharp moral and spiritual decline, yet God still had mercy on his people and raised up Judges to deliver them. The lesson for us today is that although God challenges us to be faithful to him, he extends his mercy to us just when we need it the most. What a glorious and merciful God?

CHAPTER 11

Ruth: The People of God

The Book of Ruth relates that Ruth and Orpah, two women of Moab, had married two sons of Elimelech and Noami who were Judeans and had settled in Moab to escape a famine in Judah. The husbands of all three women died and Noami planned to return to her native town Bethlehem. She urges her daughters-in-law to return to their families. Orpah returns to her family but Ruth decides to follow Noami, accepts Yahweh the God of the Israelites as her God and the Israelites as her own people. The book is a beautiful story that happens in a difficult time. It was during the time of the Judges (Ruth 1:1), When "In those days Israel had no king; everyone did as they saw fit" (Judges 21:25). Besides this lawlessness, the land was experiencing a severe famine which forced people to travel to other places for food. In these dire circumstances, it became very difficult to be God's people. The book presents a wonderful, concise and yet deep story of emptiness that turn into fullness, of despair into hope, of bitter sadness into joy and celebration. It shows how God turns around his peoples fortune. Above all, the book presents the origin of King David's royal house. The outline is simple. We see Naomi's emptiness, famine, migration, and tragedy in her family (Ruth 1:1-5).

In chapter 1:6-22, Naomi is back home with a Moabite daughter-in-law. Ruth meets Boaz whose kindness and generosity meet their need

(2:1-23). In chapter 3:1-18, Ruth and Boaz fall in love, demonstrating hope and grace in action, And in chapter 4:1-22, Ruth and Boaz marry to give fullness to Noami. All these events took place sometime between the death of Joshua around 1350 BC and David's ascension to the throne of Israel around 1,000 BC. The characters in the story are part of the story. Noami whose name means "pleasure" changed her name to Mara, early in the story because her life was quite unpleasant. Elimelech which means "God is King", was the husband of Noami from Bethleham. In those days, kings were supposed to provide for their people's needs including food and security. Yet, a great famine forced families into exile as the case was with Elimelech and Noami. Ruth, although a Moabite, became "friend" of God's people and a "refreshment" to her mother-in-law, Noami. Ruth menas "refreshment" or "friendship". Boaz means "by strength" or "with strength". He surely demonstrated great strength of character and conviction to carry on another persons- Noam's closer relatives responsibilities toward Noami. As we read through the book of Ruth, we must bear in mind that there are clear themes that the story illustrates.

- God's care and providence in the life of his people is evident in the life of Noami and Ruth.
- Loyalty, obedience and trust in God, is not limited to Israel but to other people or nations. Ruth is an example of this point.
- The story shows the ancient practice of "levirate marriage" that refers to the "husband's brother" and the redemption of property by a near relative. Boaz, although not Noami's brother-in-law, redeemed Ruth and indirectly Noami herself. Above all, during dark times of Judges, even in dire conditions of famine and suffering, God showed his presence in powerful and providential ways. He promised to give Israel the land as a sign of his fulfillment of the covenant. We see that through the story of Ruth, God arranged things so David would be born and become the seed of a new hope for his people. Through him, God's ultimate solution to the problem of sin and evil was born in the land: Jesus, the son of David, son of God, and the Redeemer of humanity.

C H A P T E R   1 2

1 & 2 Samuel: God is King but the People Want a King

The Books 1st and 2nd Samuel in the Hebrew Bible is one book of Samuel as well as 1st and 2nd Kings, and 1st and 2nd Chronicles. When the book was translated, the text was longer than the Hebrew's version. And so to make it fit better in the scrolls, the translators of the Saptuagint decided to break the book into two parts. Therefore as we read the books of Samuel, Kings and Chronicles, we shall treat then as one book each. The events the Book of Samuel presents, happened at the end of the period of the Judges around 1350-1100 BC. The Prophet Samuel was the last judge and his ministry transitioned the time of the judges to the monarchy. When the Israelites entered the Promised Land, they were a collection of tribes of the children of Israel. They hardly were the nation that God promised Abraham in Genesis 12:2. The Book of Judges tell us it was a time of lawlessness and disorder where "everyone did as they saw fit" (Judges 21:23). There was moral and spiritual decline as it is well represented by the high priest Eli and his children.

The book gives a prophetic assessment to a crucial time of Israel's history, the early era of the kings. It is meant to expose sin, warn people against rebellion, and instruct people about how God works in history. Further, it shows the beginning of the monarchy with Saul, the rise,

importance and limits of David's reign and the spiritual state of the
nation during the reign of David. The book is divided into six sections;

    (i)   Samuel: A prophet in times of transition (1 sam 1-7).

    (ii) Samuel and Saul: establishment of the monarchy in Israel (1
          Sam 8-15).

    (iii) Saul and David: Transition from Saul's failed kingdom to David
          (1 Sam 10;1-2).

    (iv) David's victorious reign over Judah and Israel (2 Sam 5:6-8:18).

    (v) David's weakness and failure as a king (2 Samuel 9-20).

    (vi) After David's reign (2 Sam 21-24).

There are many major characters that we come across as we read the
book. Below are a short sypnosis of each.

Eli was the High Priest at the town of Shiloh. Under his watch,
Samuel was born and trained. His own decline as a priest exemplified
the moral and spiritual decline of Israel at that time.

Hannah was Samuel's mother. Despite her inability to bear children,
she showed an amazing and humble faith in God. God rewarded her
with a child, Samuel. She dedicated the child to God and sang a song of
gratitude to God which is echoed by Jesus' mother, Mary in the Gospel
of Luke 1:46-55.

Samuel was God's servant who acted as Prophet, Judge and Priest for
Israel.He led the transitional period from the time of Judges to the time
of the monarchy. He anointed Saul as Israel's first King, and David, the
great King who welded the tribes of Israel into a nation.

Saul was the first King of Israel. He rebelled against God's instructions
and made serious mistakes that caused God to remove His Spirit from
upon him. Thereafter, he grew jealous of David and tried to kill him.

Jonathan was Saul's first son. He was in charge of Saul's armies.
He became David's best friend and interceded on David's behalf before
Saul. He died with his father Saul in the field of battle on Mount Gilboa.

David was the person God chose to become Saul's successor as King
of Israel. He unified the tribes of Israel into a kingdom, brought peace
to the land, and found favor with God. God made a covenant with him
to have David's descendants on the throne of Israel forever.

Bethsheba was the woman David lusted after. Although she was married to Uriah, one of David's loyal army officers, David had an affair with her and got her pregnant. Afterwards, David had her husband killed in the field of battle and married her. However the baby died because of David's sin. She later gave birth to another son called Solomon.

Nathan was the Prophet who came to David with a clever parable that denounced David's sin. David recognized his sin, repented and accepted God's punishment.

Absalom was the son of David. He led a rebellion against his father. Although at first, he succeeded, eventually he was chased out of Jerusalem and killed by the faithful generals of David.

Solomon was the son of David and Bethsheba. The Bible says the Lord loved him and because the Lord loved him, he sent word through the prophet Nathan to name him Jedidiah (2 Sam 12:24).

With this introduction of the major characters in the book of Samuel, reading through it makes it easier to understand the stories as they unfold.

The book makes it known that being God's people is a challenge to the people of Israel. Despite the warnings of Samuel, the Israelites wanted to have a king like the nations around them. God granted their request However, the monarchy turned out to be a great failure, beginning with the first king, Saul. Even though David accomplished great things, and God chose him to be the father of the future Messiah, his failures teaches us that the way of redemption of man and restoration of creation is God's own plan and no one else.

Indeed, God is King. "The Lord reigns forever and ever". (Exodus 15:18).

C H A P T E R   1 3

1 & 2 Kings: Human Limitation

———

The Book of Kings was written to provide a theological explanation for the destruction of Judah by the Babylonians in 586 BC and to provide a foundation for the return from Babylonian exile. It answers the question, "Why did God allow Israel to be taken into exile?" To understand this question, a quick overview of the history in the book is important.

In David's old age, Adonijah his son procclamied himself David's succesor. But Solomon's supportes arranged for David to procclaim Solomon as his succesor, and he comes to the throne after David's death. At the beginning of his reign, Solomon assumes God's promises to David and brings splendour to Israel and peace and prosperity to his people. The centerpiece of his reign was the building of the first temple. Eventually, Solomon follows other gods and oppresses the people of Israel. As a result of Solomon's faliure to stamp out the worship of gods other than Yahweh, the kingdom of David is split into two during the reign of Solomon's son Rehoboam who becomes the first king to reign over the Kingdom of Judah. The kings who followed Rehoboam in Jerusalem continued the royal line of David.

In the North, however, dynastys followed each other in rapid succesion and the kings were all bad for failing to follow Yahweh alone. At the end, God brings the Assyrians to destroy the Northern Kingdom in 722 BC leaving Judah as the sole custodian of the promise of God to David.

King Hezekiah, the 13th king of Judah, does what is right in the Lord's sight just as his anccestor David had done. He instituted a far reaching religous reform by centralizing sacrifice at the Temple in Jersulam and destroying the images of other gods.

God saved the Kingdom from an invasion by Assyria. But Manasseh, the next king of Judah, reverses the reforms, and God announces that he will destroy Jerusalem because of this apostasy by the King.

Manasseh's righteous grandson Josiah reinstitues the reforms of Hezekiah but it is too late. God affirms that Jerusalem shall be destroyed after the death of Josiah. In the final chapters of the book, God brings the New Babylonian Empire of King Nebuchadnezzar against Jerusalem. God withholds aid from his people; Jerusalem is raided and the Temple destroyed in 586 BC.

The priests, prophets and royal court are led to captivity. The final verse in the book records how Jehoianchin, the last King of Judah is set free and given honor by the King of Babylon (2 Kings 5:27-30).

Israel had been warned about the consequences of unfaithfulness. In the writings of Prophets such as Isaiah, or Jeremiah, we see God's warnings and judgements, as well as hopeful promises in very direct ways. But in the Book of Kings, we see a different kind of prophecy. It is a prophecy that shows rather than tells of God's warnings. It also is prophetic history because it is designed to instruct God's people about God's ways in the world. The message of the Book of Kings is based on the Torah - God's instruction to his people. There are two main lessons to learn from the Book of Kings: Kingship and Covenant - Human Kingships and Divine Kingships. In the book, human kingship is not regarded as evil but it shows that when human kings take their authority and leadership out from under the umbrella of God's own authority and leadership, they are condemned to failures. Kings, like all other God's people, must remain subjects of God's covenant. Their reign must be based on their knowlededge and submission to the Torah - God's instructions (Deuteronomy17:14-20).. The failure of the Israelites kings resulted in a divided people, a corrupted land, a polluted worship, abuse of the weak, and reliance on military power. These were symptoms of a deep spiritual disease that left the Prophet Elijah wondering if he was the last faihful follower of the Lord (1 Kings 19:14).

Divine Kingship means God is the Great King. This means, above all earthly kings and all supposedly divine kings, the Lord, the God of the Covenant with Abraham and Moses, whose presence dwelled in the Jerusalem Temple, is the King, the Creator, Owner, and Ruler of the whole creation. As such, God gave Israel a land. In this land, God provided for the needs of the people, as kings were supposed to do. He ruled and guided the people through the Torah. Also as the Great King, God rendered judgement upon the nations, including Israel itself so God ruled against Israel and Judah's unfaithfulness. As instruments of his judgemen, Assyria and Babylon conquered and exile the Northern Kingdom of Israel and the Kingdom of Judah.

The Book of Kings challenges us to be obedient and faithful to God. Our greater challenge is to trust God. Trusting God must happen at all times and in all circumstances. Trust happens over time, it requires work, and it must be exercised daily. Learning to trust Jesus as the Great King means that the values of the Kingdom of God affect every area of our lives. May the lord help us to trust him.

C H A P T E R   1 4

1 & 2 Chronicles:
The People of God

The Book of Chronicles is a book in the Hebrew Bible, found as two books (1&2 Chronicles) in the Christian Old Testament. The book was divivded into two books in the Septuagint and translated in the mid- third century BC. The first Books of the Bible, the Torah or the Pentateuch, provides an identity to the Israelites as God's people as they were about to enter the Promised Land.

Similarly, the Book of Chronicles provides an identity to the Israelites who returned from the Babylonian exile to Jerusalem. The book reviews the historical and theological continuity that exists between the pre-exilic community and the post-exilic one. The words pre-exilic, exilic and post-exilic are often used by scholars to describe three important periods in Israel's history. Pre-exilic refers to the time before 586 BC exile to Babylon. Exilic refers to the time the Israelites were in Babylon (586-539, 511 BC). And post-exilic refers to the time after the Israelites had returned to Jerusalem after 539-515 BC. They returned in three waves. The Book of Chronicles, unlike the Books of Samuel and Kings that try to explain the reasons that led to the terrible exile, wants to connect the recently arrived Jews to their history. The promise and hope for a restored Israel is found in the ancient history of the people, a history that the Jews must remember, understand, and make their own. Through genealogies, remembered history, connected with the Davidic Kingdom and covenant, and God's activities in Israel, especially in Judah, Chronicles identifies what it means to be God's people once again in the land. Even though it is a hopeful time, it is still a time of uncertainty. Israel is not a kingdom or a nation because it is a vassal region of the Persian Empire. The land where the returning Jews dwell is a city, Jerusalem, a destroyed city without walls or a Temple. However, the returned Jews were direct historical and spiritual descendants of ancient Israel, especially of the David line.

The Book has three divisions:

(i) The genealogies in Chapters 1-9 of 1st Chronicles.
(ii) The reigns of David and Solomon constituting the reminder of 1 Chronicles, and Chapters 1-9 of 2 Chronicles.
(iii) The narrative of the divided kingdom, focusing on the Kingdom of Judah in the remainder of 2 Chronicles.

The history the Chronicler has narrated is a warning against complacency, rebellion, and idolatry. The monarchy cannot be successful without God as the true King. The words of the Prophets are God's warning system to his people; they must carefully be heard. The instructions in the Torah are more than empty rituals; they teach God's people how to approach and please the King. It teaches us that God's warning to Israel's unfaithfulness are not empty words or threats. Surely, God punishes rebellion.

There are five themes that the Book of Chronicles highlights. These themes are a theological reflection, not a "history of Israel". The first is that God is active in history, especially the history of Israel. The faithfulness or sins of individual kings are immediately rewarded or punished by God.

Second, God calls Israel to a special relationship. The call begins with genealogies, gradually narrowing the focus from all mankind to a single family, the Israelites, the descendants of Jacob.

The third is that God chose David and his dynasty as the agents of his will. According to the author of Chronicles, the three great events of

David's reign were his bringing the Ark of the Covenant to Jerusalem, his founding of an eternal royal dynasty, and his preparations for the construction of the Temple.

The fourth, God chose a site in Jerusalem as the location of the Temple, the place where God should be worshiped. By stressing the central role of the Temple in pre-exilic Judah, Chronicles also stresses the importance of the newly rebuilt second temple to his readers. Lastly, Chronicles reminds readers that God remains active in Israel. The past is used to legitimize the author's present: this is seen most clearly not only in the detailed attention he gives to the temple built by Solomon, but also in the genealogy and lineages which connects his own generation to the distant past and thus makes the claim that the present is a continuation of the past.

Therefore, what we learn from the Book of Chronicles is the faithfulness of God. He was faithful to Israel in the past and he would be again in their time. They returned with the protection and permission of the Persian king, but they knew that God brought them back to Jerusalem. We also learn that kingship was important. The kings were central in the life of Israel until the exile. The Israelites were no longer a nation, so they did not have a king.Yet, their history told them that God was their King, and he had promised that one day a human king would sit on the throne of David, restore Israel, defeat its enemies, and bring Israel into God's peace. That promise of the coming of the Messiah, is a central hope in the book. King David is also showcased in the Book of Chronicles: David's kingship and God's covenant with him. His kingship is looked to as a source of hope and continuity. The covenant between God and David is the basis for creating a new community of restored Jews in Jerusalem. The last two points are about the Temple and the unity of Israel. The Temple was important because it was the visible representation of God's presence. It dominated the view on Mt. Zion, and reminded Israel that God's presence with them was a sign of his faithfulness to the covenant and the fulfillment of his promises. The unity of Israel is stressed because as a group of Jews returned to Jerusalem, there were no longer two nations in opposition to each other (Israel and Judah). They were just one people in one city struggling to survive, rebuild, and find identity as God's people. Therefore, the unity of the people and the promises of restoration of all Israel were central to that community. Chronicles reminds us that God began to fulfill his promise to restore Israel by bringing them back from exile. Therefore, the ending anticipates a time that goes back to David's kingdom, with Israel once again a united people in the Promised Land.

Today, in Jesus, God showed his intention to restore humanity as a whole through David's descendant, the Messiah, God's son. Jesus is the fulfillment of that ancient promise to save humanity from the bondage of sin, restore them to a relationship with God and renew their hearts and minds.

"If my people, who are called by my name, will humble themselves and pray and seek my face and turn from their wicked way, then I will hear from heaven, and I will forgive their sin and will heal their land" (2 Chronicles 7:14).

Ezra & Nehemiah: Faith Under Seige

The Book of Ezra & Nehemiah covers the period from the fall of Babylon in 539 BC to the second half of the 5th Century BC, and it tells of the successive missions to Jerusalem of Zerubbabel, Ezra, and Nehemiah and their efforts to restore the worship of the God of Israel and to create a purified Jewish community. The book covers almost a century of history, Ezra, and Nehemiah, and their efforts to restore the worship of the God of Israel and to create a purified Jewish community. Ezra chapter 1-7 covers the period from 537-515 BC and Ezra chapter 7-Nehemiah 13 covers 458-433 BC.

The setting of the book is very interesting. Because of Israel's unfaithfulness, God punished Israel. in 722 BC, the Assyrians conquered and exiled the Northern Kingdom of Israel.

In 586 BC, the Babylonians destroyed and exiled the Southern Kingdom of Judah. Babylon itself was destroyed by the Persian King Cyrus in 539 BC. Ezra and Nehemiah mentioned four Persian kings: Cyrus who reigned between 559-530 BC; Darius I (521-486 BC), Xerxes I (485-465 BC), and Artaxerxes I (465-424 BC). These kings expanded the Persian Empire westward, including Egypt and parts of Greece. The power and influence of the empire lasted until 330 BC, when the

Macedonian Alexander the Great defeated the Persian armies and entered the cities of Susa and Persepolis.

Cyrus the Great re-organized the Persian empire into administrative provinces or districts. Jerusalem was part of the Arabian province. After praying to God, Nehemiah, a cupbearer of the Persian king. Artaxerxes I, requested permission and support from the king to return and rebuild the walls of Jerusalem. The king granted his request and named him governor of Judea and Jerusalem the administrative center of the region.

The story of Ezra and Nehemiah allows us to see the precarious life the Jews in Jerusalem led. The dangers were more than just physical: the very existence of the community as a remnant of God's people was in danger. Ezra and Nehemiah responded to these with very concrete and immediate physical, social, political and spiritual needs. Unlike the Israelites who entered the Promised Land many centuries ago under Joshua's leadership, the Jews who came back from exile to Jerusalem were not a conquering army. Rather, they were a religious community of builders who first built the temple, then the city walls, and in the process, the community itself. It was a community in constant danger from outside. They faced opposition to building the Temple of the Lord and rebuilding the walls of the city, and from inside, they faced the threats of rebellion and apathy. The book follows the pattern of the royal court of Persia that authorizes them to rebuild the temple, then there is a journey, opposition, and success.

Ezra and Nehemiah look at this history with the eyes of faith and discern God's actions in their time. The actions of the Persian king are, infact God's own actions. More specifically, the book relates the life and death struggle the community experienced to fulfill its calling to build. The restored community of Jerusalem experienced a social and spiritual siege. At stake was not the land or political power, but rather spiritual faithfulness to God. And Ezra and Nehemiah led the way to victory. As God's people, and as a community of builders, they learned, to survive in their unstable situation, while hoping for a more complete restoration of Israel's good fortunes. The book of Ezra and Nehemiah show the fulfillment of God's promises to restore Israel. However, the promise was only pertailly fulfilled. The complete fulfillment of God's promise occured in Jesus Christ the Lord.

CHAPTER 16

Esther: Courage in Challenging Times

The Book of Esther relates the story of a Hebrew woman in person born as Hadassah but known as Esther, who becomes Queen of Persia and thwarts a genocide of her people. The story forms the core of the Jewish festival of Purin, during which it is read aloud twice; once in the evening and again in the following morning. The Book of Esther is set in person in the Capital Susa in the third year of the reign of the Persian king Ahasuerus also known as Xerxes who ruled between 486 and 465 BC. The story of Esther is that king Ahasuerus, ruler of the Perian Empire, holds a lavish 180-day banquet, initially for his court and dignitaries and afterwards a seven-day banquet for all the inhabitants of the capital city, Susa (Esther 1:1-9). On the seventh day of the latter banquet, king Ashasuerus orders the Queen, Vasti, to display her beauty before the guests by coming before them wearing her crown (1:10-11).

She refuses, infuriating the king who on the advice of his counselors removes her from her position as an example to other women who might be emboldemed to disobey their husbands (1:12-19). A decree follows that "every man should be ruler in his own house" (1:20-22). Ahasuerus then makes arrangement to choose a new queen from a selection of beautiful young women from throughout the empire (2:1-4). Among those women is a Jewish orphan named Esther, who was raised by her Uncle Mordecai (2:5-7). She finds favor in the kings eyes, and is crowded his new queen, but she does not reveal her Jewish heritage (2:8-20). Shortly afterwards, Mordecai discovers that a plot by two courtiers, Bigthan and Teresh, to assassinate the king. The conspirators are arrested and hanged, and Mordecai's service to the king is recorded (2:21-23). Ahasuerus appoints Haman as his viceroy (3:1). Mordecai who sits at the palace gates, falls into Haman's disfavor as he refuses to bow down to him (3:2-5). Haman discovers that Mordecai refuses to bow on account of his Jewishness, and in revenge, plots to kill not only Moerdecai but all the Jews in the empire (3:6). He obtains Ahasuerus's persmission to execute this plan against payment of ten thousand talents of silver, and cast lots "purim" to choose the date on which to do this - the thirteenth of the month of Adar (3:7-12). A royal degree is issued throughout the kingdom to slay all Jews on that date (3:13-15). When Mordecai discovers the plan, he goes into mourning and implores Esther to intercede with the king (4:1-5). But she is afraid to present herself to the king unsummoned, an offense punishable by death (4:6-12). Instead, she directs Mordecai to have all Jews fast for three days for her, and vows to fast as well (4:15-16). On the third day, she goes to Ahasuerus, who stretches out his sceptre to her to indicate that she is not to be punished (5:1-2). She invites him to a feast in the company of Haman (5:3-5). During the feast, she asks them to attend a further feast the next evening (5:6-8). Meanwhile, Haman is again offended by Mordecai and at his wife's suggestion, has a gallow built to hang Mordecai (5:9-14). That night, the king could not sleep, and orders the court records to be read to him (6:1). He is reminded that Mordecai interceded in the previous plot against his life, and discovers that Mordecai never received any recognition (6:4-3). Just then, Haman appears to request the king's permission to hang Mordecai, but before he can make this request, Ahasuerus asks Haman what should be done for the man that the king wished to honor (6:4-6). Assuming that the king was referring to Haman himself, Haman suggests that the man be dressed in the king's royal robes and crown and led around on the kings royal horse, while a herald calls. "See how the king honors a man he wishes to reward" (6:7-9). To his surprise and horror, the king instructs Haman to do so to Mordecai (6:10-11). Immediately after, Ahasuerus and Haman attend Esther's second banquet. The king promises to grant her any request, and she reveals that she is a Jewish and Haman is planning to exterminate her people, including herself (7:1-6).

Overcome with rage, the king leaves the room; meanwhile Haman stays behind and begs Esther for his life, falling upon her in desperation (7:7).

The king returns at this very moment and thinks Haman is assaulting the queen; this makes him angrier and he orders Haman hanged on the very gallows that Haman had prepared for Mordecai (7:8-10). Unable to annul a formal royal decree, the king instead adds to it, permitting the Jews to join together and destroy any and all those seeking to destroy them.

On the 13 of Adar, Haman's ten sons and other ñmen are killed in Susa (9:1-12). Upon hearing this, requested it to be repeated the next day, whereupon 300 more men are killed (9:13-15). More than 75,000 people are killed by Jews who are careful to take no plunder (9:16-17). Mordecai and Esther send letters throughout all the provinces instituting an annual commemoration of the Jewish people's redemption in a holiday called Purim. (9:20-28).

The king remains very powerful and continues his reign with Mordecai assuming a prominent position in his court (10:1-3).

God promises to be with his people (Gen. 28:15; Ex. 33:14; Isa. 43:2; Matt. 28:20). The Book of Esther shows that although God is apparently absent in the story, his protection is ever present with his people. Faith is active. God expects us to exercise our faith, as Esther did, especially in times of danger, uncertainty, or suffering. The activity is not moved by "blind faith". Rather, by a faith that knows God to be present, powerful and willing to act on our behalf. That is the story of the Book of Esther.

C H A P T E R   1 7

The Poetry and Wisdom Books

This section of the Old Testament is called the Books of Wisdom and Poetry.

This section three of the Old Testament is called the Books of Wisdom and Poetry.

There are five books in this section: Job, Psalms, Proverbs, Ecclesiastes and Song of Songs. They follow the Torah/ Pentetauch and the Historical Books.

The fascinating narratives of the Pentetauch and the Historical Books as we have seen, tell the story of the people of Israel from creation of the world to their settlement in the land of Canaan, their defeat by foreign nations, their exile, and their return from exile in Babylon.

The Books of Wisdom and Poetry are a completely different type of literature from these narratives. The Books in this section include excellent examples of Hebrew poetry, characterized by repetition of words and parallelism and by patterns of rhythm. While some of these books fall into the category of wisdom writing like Job, Ecclesiastes and Proverbs, the others are collections of love poems (Song of Songs) or worship prayers and songs (Psalms).

The Books of Wisdom writings explore important questions about life and give advice for practical living, especially in community with others. However, these writings make it clear that true wisdom is a gift that comes from God who gives helpful advice to everyone who obeys God's Law. For example, these verses summarize two important understanding of wisdom found in the Hebrew Scriptures: first, true wisdom comes from God (Proverbs 2:6-7), second, God offers wisdom and guidance for daily life(

Proverbs 6:23). The writer of Psalm 1 puts it this way:

"Blessed is the man who does not walk in the counsel of the wicked or stand in the way of sinners or sit in the seat of mockers. But his delight is in the law of the Lord, and on his law he meditates day and night". (Psalm 1:1-2).

The story of Job focuses on the question: " Why do innocent people suffer?".

Ecclesiastes on the other hand, focuses on the question of finding meaning in life.

Proverbs celebrates human wisdom and wisdom that comes from God's Law as the way to a happy and prosperous life.

The Books of Poetry are written entirely in poetic form. Song of Songs is a beautiful example of Hebrew poetry. It was originally written as a love poem to describe the joy and extreme happiness of two people in love. But it also has been understood in some Jewish traditions as a description of God's love for Israel and in some Christian traditions as a description of Christ's love for the Church.

The Book of Psalm is named after the Greek word "psalmos" which means "song". The songs and prayers found in the Book of Psalm were therefore used by the Hebrew people to express their relationship with God. The Psalms cover a whole range of human emotions: from joy to anger, and from hope to despair.

We shall look at these books more closely in the chapters that follow.

CHAPTER 18

Job: God's People and Suffering

———

The Book of Job is one of the most celebrated pieces of Biblical literature not only because it explores some of the most profound questions humans ask about their lives, but also because it is extremely well written.

The Book looks at the problem of human suffering and concludes that to deal with suffering, believers do not need knowledge but trust.

It is the story of a just man who, unaware of the conversation happening in the celestial court between God and Satan, finds his life overthrown. His painful experience and intense conversations invite us to reflect about suffering and justice.

The Book opens with a scene in heaven where Satan comes to accuse Job before God. He insists that Job only serves God because God protects him and seeks God's permission to test Job's faith and loyalty. God grants his permission only within certain boundaries.

"Why do the righteous suffer? is the question raised after Job loses his family, wealth, and his health.

Job's three friends Eliphaz, Bildad, and Zopher, come to comfort him and to discuss his crushing series of tragedies. They insist his suffering is punishment for sin in his life. Job, though, remains devoted to God through all of this and contends that his life has not been one of sin. A fourth man, Elihu, tells Job he needs to humble himself and submit to God's use of trials to purify his life.

Finally, Job questions God Himself and learns valuable lessons about the sovereignty of God and his need to totally trust in the Lord. Job is then restored to health, happiness, and prosperity beyond his earlier state.

The Book of Job reminds us that there is a "cosmic conflict" going on behind the scenes that we usually know nothing about. Often, we wonder why God allows something, and we question or doubt God's goodness without seeing the full picture. The Book teaches us to trust God, not only when we do not understand, but because we do not understand. The Psalmist tells us : " As for God, His way is perfect"(Psalm 18: 30). If God's ways are perfect, then we can trust that whatever he allows is also perfect. This may not seem possible to us, but our minds are not God's mind. It is true that we cannot expect to understand His mind perfectly as he reminds us. "For my thoughts are not your thoughts, neither are your ways my ways,says the LORD. For as the heavens are higher than the earth, so are my ways and thoughts than your thoughts" (Isaiah 55:8-9).

Therefore, our responsibility to God is to obey Him, trust Him, and to submit to His will whether we understand it or not. God created all things. He is in control of the universe. Most often, we cannot see or understand his role behind the scenes. However, God want us to trust in His wisdom, his goodness and his plans. That is the message from the Book of Job.

The Psalms: God's Presence in Songs and Prayers

The Book of Psalm is a compilation of many songs, by many authors over a long period of time.It is a book of songs and prayers for God's people. The Psalms provide us with the vocabulary of God's people for worship. Because the Psalms are poems, they have a wonderful way to express the deepest emotions of our hearts. Whether in times of suffering and sadness or joy or celebration, the Psalms have been close to God's people at all times and places.

In addition, the Psalms is a book of instruction. It is divided into five books, just like the Torah/ Pentetauch, a book that instructs us what it means to be God's people. However, the Psalms do not give instructions about how to pray and praise God. Rather, the Psalms show us how to do it.

Lastly, the Psalms express God's people's longing for the coming Messiah. God has promised through his prophets that a descendant of King David would always sit on the throne of Israel. Although the Psalms are not prophecies in the same sense as the Prophetic Books, they do anticipate, so they speak prophetically about the coming Messiah.

The Book of Psalms is divided into five sections, each closing with a doxology or a benediction.

> Book 1 consist of Psalms 1-41..
> Book 2 consist of Psalms 42-72.
> Book 3 consist of Psalms 73-89.
> Book 4 consist of Psalms 90-106.
> Book 5 consist of Psalms 197-150.

Book 1 is dominated by Prayers of lament and expressions of confidence in God.

Book 2 is full of communal laments and ends with royal palms.

Book 3 the prayers of laments and distress are more intense and bleak.

Book 4 presents the answers to bleakness of book 3. The theme " The Lord Reigns" dominated this book.

Book 5 declares that God is in control, will redeem his people, and praises God's faithfulness and goodness.

Curiously, the Psalms of lament outnumber any other type of Psalm. This fact might reflect the chaos of life, the many reasons for suffering and sadness.

However, the Psalms do not typically end in lament. They move from lament to praise, from grief to joy. The conclusion of the Psalms, the magnificent hallelujah songs of 146-150, reflect that with God, all tears will be dried, all suffering will turn to joy, and all injustices will receive the proper and righteous response.

As we read through the Book of Psalms, we will come across many themes such as: The Lord Reigns, Creation, Salvation, Judgement, God's people, and the King.

One of the greatest lesson we learn from the Book of Psalms is that no matter who or what claims control over creation, God is the rightful and just ruler of all Psalms 47, 93 and 95-99 offer a splendid and beautiful account of the claim that the Lord Reigns.

God promised in the Old Testament that he will be with his people. In times of suffering and trouble, it always seems God has turned his face away from his people. However, the songs of petition, lament, and praise show that God has always been faithful to his word. He answers the requests of his people because he is a good, powerful, and compassionate God.

And humanity's ultimate plight, sin and death, will finally be answered through the Messiah.

Today, the Messiah, Jesus Christ, has come and has defeated sin and death.Yet we still live in a world filled with trials, temptations, and suffering. However, the songs of petition, lament and praise in the Psalms invite us to trust that God is always present, that he reigns over all, and he will intervene in the perfect time with the perfect answers to our needs.

Read the Book of Psalms for inspiration, hope and joy. You will love it.

CHAPTER 20

Proverbs: A Guide to Holy Living

The Book of Proverbs is an anthology of different authors who wrote at different times. Proverbs 1:1, 10:1, and 25:1 affirm that King Solomon was the main author. Proverbs 25:1 also affirms that the " men of Hezekiah king of Judah" copied them. The Book also recognizes other contributors: wise men (22:17; 24:23), Agur (30:1), and Lemuel (31:1). However, nothing is known about these writers.

As a collection, the book was written in a span from the 900 BC to the 700 BC period. The purpose of the book is to persuade and instruct God's people to gain wisdom. It invites readers to make a decision. The choice is not only a rational one, it involves desires and emotions, as well as intelligence and discernment. The Book attempts to capture the reader's will by appealing to the imagination. It invites us to make a life- changing choice by choosing wisdom over folly. The readers hear from both Lady Wisdom and Lady Folly. Their invitations become alternatives between life and death.The introduction states its own purpose:

"for gaining wisdom and instruction; for understanding words of insight; for receiving instruction in prudent behavior, doing what is right and just and fair" (Proverbs 1:2-3).

The whole Book of Proverbs, presents an appeal to choose wisdom over all things. Wisdom, the book stresses is created by God (8:22-23}, God reveals to us the source of wisdom (2:6-7; 39: 5-6), the beginning of wisdom is " the fear of the Lord" (1:7; 2;5; 8:10; 14:27), and lastly, wisdom is desirable over all things (4:7-9; 8:19-11).

Concerning humanity, Proverbs is an invitation to accurately identify the source of all wisdom and the limit of human wisdom:

Humans are created by God (29:13),

Humans delude themselves (12:15; 14:12, 28:26).

The heart is central and reveals humanity's true character (27:19), and Humans are are inherently foolish(22:15).

The Book of Proverbs gives a description of a wise man by stressing that wisdom is not something easily taught. As with many things, it is easier to show what a wise person looks like than describe wisdom. Wise people are recognized by their character (13:5-6), by their loyalty (16:6), by their humility (2:5,9), they are teachable (12:1), have self-control and not rash(17:27), forgiving (10:12), thoughtful (13:16), honest (12:22), do not boast (27:2), do not slander (6:13), and are peaceful (12:6).

Wise people value their relationship with their spouse - they recognize that their spouse is from God (18:22), acknowledge their spouse as their crowning glory (12:4), and are faithful to their spouse (5:15-20).

Wise people value their relationship with their children- they acknowledge the need for wisdom in their children's lives (Proverbs 1-9), recognize their children's natural condition (22:5), understand children can be guided (19:18), and they live and discipline them (13:24).

Wise people care about their relationship with other people– they choose kind friends (22:24-25), value and are loyal to their friends (27:19), behave fairly and justly with all (3:27-28), are considerate (25:17), and live in peace with all (3:29).

Wise people value possession– they recognize the proper value of money (30:7-9), honor God with their possessions and recognize that blessings come from God (3:9-10), recognize that foolish behavior leads to poverty (6:6-11), as do injustice and oppression (13:23, 16:8, 22:16), they are generous with possessions (3:27-28), and are kind to animals (12:10).

Lastly, the theme of Kingship runs through the Book of Proverbs. In the world of ancient Israel, the king represented the people. Kings were meant to model attitudes, behaviors, and character that all people should display in their lives. Jesus, the King of kings, plays this role when he shows us what it means to be God's children. Thus, the King, knows his place (21:1), is wise (8:15-16), is righteous (25:5), is just (27:8), have self-control (31:1-7), is compassionate (31:8-9), and is surrounded by godly people (16:13, 22:11).

As we read through the Book of Proverbs, we will see that Proverbs raises questions of value, moral behavior, the meaning of human life and righteous conduct. And we are challenged to discover and model our lives based on the principles outlined about wise people.

C H A P T E R 2 1

Ecclesiastes: Searching for Truth and Meaning

The Book of Ecclesiastes is presented as a biography of Qoheleth-Teacher/ Preacher. His story is framed by the voice of the narrator who refers to Qoheleth in the third person, praises his wisdom but remindsAa the reader that wisdom has it's limitations and is not man's main concern.

After the introduction in Chapter 1:2-11, comes the words of Qoheleth the Preacher. As King, he has experienced everything and done everything, but concludes that nothing is ultimately reliable, as death levels all. The Preacher states that the only good is to partake of life in the present, for enjoyment is from the hand of God. Everything is ordered in time and people are subject to time in contrast to God's eternal character. The world is filled with injustice, which only God will adjudicate. God and humans do not belong in the same realm, and it is therefore necessary to have a right attitude before God. People should enjoy, but should not be greedy; no one knows what is good for humanity; righteousness and wisdom escape humanity.

The Preacher reflects on the limits of human power: all people face death, and death is better than life, but people should enjoy life when they can, for a time may come when no one can. The world is full of risk the Preacher says and gives advice on living with risk, both political and economic. He finishes with imagery of nature languishing and humanity marching to the grave.

The subjects of Ecclesiastes are the pain and frustration engendered by observing and meditating on the distortions and inequities pervading the world, the uselessness of human ambition, and the limitations of worldly wisdom and righteousness. In connection with these observations, all this coexists with a firm belief in God whose power, justice, and unpredictability are sovereign.

The book's conclusion is : A meaningful, fulfilling, and joyous life is not found in the frivolous pursuit of wealth, success and pleasure. Instead, meaning and fulfillment is found when we pursue God as our number one priority— trusting and obeying God in all circumstances. Simply put, the world " under the sun" is meaningless apart from God.

To us who live today, the end for the search for truth and meaning is Jesus Christ. Seeking worldly pleasures, wealth or power will not lead to righteousness and salvation. Only seeking Christ and believing in his death and resurrection will find righteousness, salvation and true meaning. " Now this is eternal life: that they may know you, the only true God, and Jesus Christ, whom you have sent" (John 17:3).

Song of Songs: The Love Song

Son of Songs is a book that celebrates marital love. The descriptions in the book, both of characters and their desire for each other, are filled with passionate and creative language. It portrays love and desire as something that is good and fulfilling, without guilt or shame. It gently displays the emotion involved in losing love, and provides a strong, repeated warning to not enter into this love before the proper time (Song 2:7, 3:5, 8:4).

"Song of Songs" means the best of all songs, like "King of kings" or " Lord of Lord's". The Book is also known as the Song of Solomon. The first three chapters is a poetic declaration of mutual love and affection between both lover and his beloved. Moving from courtship to wedding ceremony and banquet, Song of Songs emphasizes the beauty, passion, and intimacy found within marriage. The book illustrates the love that should exist between husband and wife.

Although the title identifies King Solomon as the author (1:1), the different poems within the book seem to have been written by different authors similar to the book of Psalms.

The book stresses that joy, passion, and intimacy, and authentic love can exist within the gift of marriage and we can experience joy, passion and intimacy in a loving relationship with God.

In short, love, intimacy, and marriage are gifts from God and that love, passion, and intimacy found within the context of marriage are part of God's design.

The Apostle Paul wrote, " Husbands, love your wives, just as Christ loved the Church and gave himself up for her" (Ephesians 5:25). The Church is the bride of Christ. As Christ's bride, we are his beloved and we participate in a loving, passionate, and intimate relationship with him. Song of Songs, although not primarily an allegory of our relationship with Jesus, it is a good example of a loving relationship with our Lord and Savior.

C H A P T E R   2 3

The Prophetic Books

The Prophetic Books are the last section of the Old Testament. They are records of the Prophetic ministry of individuals whom God called and sent to encourage, warn, exhort and guide his people— Israel. These books are divided into two sections: the Major and Minor Prophets.

In Biblical times, Biblical books were written in scrolls and had a size limit. All the twelve Minor Prophets fit well into one scroll, so they became one unit. The Major Prophets were much longer but both the Major and Minor Prophets were the same type of Prophetic literature.

The terms " major" or " minor" have nothing to do with the achievement or the importance of the Prophets, rather, the length of the books. In comparison to the books of the twelve Minor Prophets, whose books were short and grouped together into one single book in the Hebrew Bible, the Major Prophets are books that are much longer.

The Books of the Major Prophets are: Isaiah, Jeremiah, Lamentations, Ezekiel and Daniel. The Minor Prophets are: Hosea,, Joel, Amos, Obadiah, Jonah, Micah, Nahum, Habakkuk, Zephaniah, Haggai, Zechariah and Malachi.

Now, the question is: What is prophecy?

Prophecy is a message that has been communicated to a prophet by God to his people. Prophets in Biblical times, were God's servants specifically called to be his witnesses. In the Old Testament, prophecy was a tool used by God to communicate his will to his people. Prophets were not only teachers of the law which was the main duty of the priest as recorded in Deuteronomy 33:10 but God sent Prophets to his people during times of crisis such as:

1. During times of military threats against God's people (Isaiah 36-37).
2. When the people rebelled against God's will (Genesis 3:11-19, Ezekiel 2:3-5).
3. When hope seemed all but lost (Jeremiah 28:11).
4. And when the people needed comfort in difficult times (Isaiah 49:1-5).

The Old Testament Prophets were therefore, intermediaries between God and his people. They stood in the gap that separates God from humans. They brought the Word of God to the people, and interceded on behalf of the people before God. Amos 3:7 says: " Surely the Sovereign Lord does nothing without revealing his plans to his servants the prophet".

Very often, prophecy dealt with current issues to the prophet's time but in Biblical times, God also revealed the future to his prophets.

If we read through all the Prophetic Books, we will find the following main themes:

1. ONE TRUE GOD.
   Only the Lord, the God of
   Abraham,
   Issac and Jacob is the true God
   and Creator of the universe. All
   other claims to divinity are false.

2. GOD IS HOLY
   The very being of God is holiness. God's holiness means that he is not part of nature but is it's creator. God is beyond his creation. For this reason, any attempt to make an image of him becomes an idolatry. Because of his holiness, he does not tolerate

sin. Sin offends him because it is opposite of what he desires for his creation..

3. GOD IS SOVEREIGN
    As the Creator of all things, God
    rules and owns it all. The best
    image to express this truth is that
    God is King. Yet because he is
    beyond the created world and our own experience, God is much
    more than a king. He is the King of the nations and his people.

4. GOD IS MERCIFUL AND FULL OF GRACE.
    Even though God is holy and sovereign, he is interested in his
    creation and in humanity. He is involved in what humans do
    and do not do. His willingness to send Prophets to correct,
    warn, comfort and guide his people shows his interest. Mercy
    and grace are also part of his nature.

5. GOD IS JUST AND GOOD
    Because God is merciful, he has shown amazing patience with
    his people and faithfulness to his covenant. The prophets made
    it clear that God wishes his people to be obedient and repentant,
    and wishes to forgive and transform them. Yet he will punish
    and discipline them in love when necessary.

6. THE TORAH
    The Prophets alluded, quoted, enforced and applied the law of
    Moses to specific events, persons and circumstances.

7. THE COVENANT
    God's activities, both his promises of restoration and his acts of
    judgement, come from his faithfulness to his covenant.

8. THE EXILE AND RESTORATION
    The exile to Assyria of the Northern Kingdom in 722 BC and
    to Babylon around 586 BC of the Southern Kingdom, became
    the a central theme. The Prophets warned, called to repent,

announced judgement upon Israel, and explained the reasons for the exile. They also comforted the people with assurance that God would save and restore them.

9.   THE MESSIAH
In all, the central component of the Prophets' announcement of salvation was the coming of a special person who will represent, save and restore Israel.

As we read through these prophetic books, let us be mindful of those themes and we will understand better the messages of each book. In the next chapter, we shall study the Major Prophets. Enjoy this last section of the Old Testament.

C H A P T E R   2 4

Isaiah: God's Judgement
and Salvation

————

Isaiah the Prophet was the son of Amos.

(1:1). He was married and had two children. He lived at the time of Amos, Hosea, and Micah. He prophesized and wrote during the reign of Uzziah, Jotham, Ahaz and Hezekiah, King of Judah. He was called to prophesy to the Kingdom of Judah and he preached a message of judgement and salvation.

The background story is that Judah formed many political and military alliances in hopes of protecting itself from powerful enemies on all sides of Judah and war looming. Isaiah opposed these alliances because they showed Judah's reliance upon human power over divine power. Isaiah knew that any alliance with a world power would place Judah in submission as a vassal to the powerful nation. This would lead Judah to serve the gods of those states because vassal states during Isaiah's time, usually adopted the religions of the overlords.

The Prophet Isaiah, therefore, exhorted Judah and her kings to seek God and maintain their faith in God's providence and faithfulness rather than trusting military and political strength of other nations. He stressed that God would save and deliver Judah If they trusted God to do so. But if Judah continue to doubt God, then Judah will meet the same fate as the Northern Kingdom of Israel which Assyria conquered and sent to exile.

Also, Isaiah was outraged by the idolatry, injustice, rebellion, distain, unrighteousness and scandalous behavior of God's people and communicated God's anger, disappointment and sorrow with his people's behavior and warn them of impending judgement.

He warned Judah saying if they continue to turn to political treaties, other gods, and military strength to save them their efforts to do so would prove useless. Unless the people of Judah repented and fully relied on God as their savior, they would never be safe from destruction.

Isaiah was more than a prophet of doom. He wrote prophecies of hope and salvation. His prophecies anticipates the coming of a king, a Messiah who will fulfill all of God's promises to Israel. A remnant of God's people will find their redemption in the coming Messiah– a suffering servant— who will die to save them.

To understand the predicament of Judah's reliance on foreign nations during Isaiah's time, let us look at a short history of the situation at that time. In 745 BC, Tiglath Pileser III, King of Assyria began to expand the Assyrian Empire westward. As he threatened the borders of many small kingdoms, they frequently formed coalitions to fight the advancing armies.

In 733 BC, Syrian King Rezin and King Pejah of Israel formed a coalition. When King Ahaz of Judah refused to join them, Syria and Israel, the Northern Kingdom, attacked Judah. Instead of trusting in God's providence, Ahaz formed an alliance with Assyria and thus became a vassal state of Assyria. As a result, Ahaz had to appear before the King of Assyria Tiglath Pileser III to pay homage to the Assyrian God.

Then in 722 BC, Israel the Northern Kingdom fell to the Assyrians and Southern Kingdom of Judah continued to struggle with the consequences of their alliance with Assyria and later an alliance with Babylonia and Egypt. This is what in the long ministry of Isaiah, he warned the kings of Judah about the political and military deals as well as their unrighteousness, complacency, injustices and arrogance. But they did not listen. Eventually, Judah was conquered in 586 BC by the Neo Babylonia empire for failing to pay taxes and for rebellion against Babylon.

In the Book of Isaiah, there are some common themes that we need to take note of because they ran through the book.

1. GOD THE HOLY ONE OF ISRAEL.
    This means God is a Holy God, and he will not tolerate sin. Sin will be punished. We see this illustrated in the conquest of Israel the Northern Kingdom in 722 BC and eventually, Judah in 586 BC.

2. GOD AS SAVIOR AND REDEEMER.
    God is a merciful, loving, forgiving God. Israel and Judah deserved to be completely destroyed because of their sin of idolatry, rebellion, and disobedience to God, but God promised salvation and restoration to a remnant.

3. THE PROMISED MESSIAH– GOD'S SUFFERING SERVANT.
    Only through the suffering of the promised Messiah, God's servant, will God's people be healed and forgiven of their sins. The promised Messiah through his suffering, will inaugurate the Kingdom of God— the new heaven and the new earth.

The book of Isaiah teaches us some valuable lessons in our relationship with God. First we must look at ourselves in the mirror and our relationship with God.

So often we place our trust in money, possessions, weapons, governments, or our leaders. We form alliances, or sacrifice our integrity instead of trusting in God's provision and providence. Well, the book of Psalms reminds us that God is our Rock, our Fortress, our Deliverer, our Shield, and our Salvation (Psalm 18:2).

When we are in trouble, God assures us that " Those who hope in the Lord will renew their strength. They will soar on wings like eagles; they will run and not grow weary, they will walk and not faint" (Isaiah 40:31).

Let us not make the mistake that Israel and Judah made.Trust in the Lord always. He will deliver and protect you says the Prophet Isaiah.

CHAPTER 25

Jeremiah: Judgement, Doom, and Weeping.

Jeremiah was an active Prophet during the reigns of Josiah, Jehoiakim, Johoiachin and Zedekiah, kings of Judah. He received his call in 626 BC and wrote his prophecies until about 582 BC. His message is intended as a message to the Jews in exile in Babylon, explaining the disaster of exile as God's response to Israel's pagan worship. Jeremiah says the people are like unfaithful wife and rebelliousness made judgement inevitable, although restoration and a new covenant are foreshadowed.

During Isaiah's time, King Hezekiah of Judah (716--687 BC) made several reforms and sought more independence for Judah. When the Assyrian King Sennacher attacked Judah, God saved Jerusalem. The people of Judah believed that the Tepmple and Jerusalem could never be destroyed. This belief known as "inviolability Zion", gave the people a lazy attitude towards obeying God. However under Hezekiah's son, King Manasseh (697-647 BC), Judah became a loyal vassal state to Assyria. The next two Assyrian kings Esarhaddon (680-669 BC) and Ashurbanipal (668-627 BC), conquered Egypt and eventually sacked the ancient Egyptian capital of Thebes in 664 BC. This signaled the rise of the Assyrian Empire. As a result, King Manasseh of Judah under the Assyrian Empire as a vassal state, instituted pagan worship, supported sacred prostitution in the Temple area, and human sacrifice. Manasseh's evil doings contributed greatly to the fall of Judah.

Meanwhile, Assyria expanded its borders too far and had difficulty maintaining control. Thus it began to weaken on all sides. Then in 628 BC, Manasseh's grandson, Josiah (641-609 BC), began to make sweeping reforms. It was shortly after this reform that Jeremiah started his ministry. At this time, the Babyl onians grew in power, and the King of Babylon Nabopolassar (625-605 BC) sacked the Assyrian capital of Nineveh and conquered it in 612 BC. Thereafter, Assyria was never a major world empire.

In 609 BC, King Josiah was killed by Pharaoh Necho II. King Josiah's son Johoiachin was placed on the throne of Judah. He did not maintain the policies and reforms of his father. In this context, Jeremiah began his ministry in Jerusalem and preached judgement, doom and called on his people to repent. He brought a message of judgement against the people of Judah with the hope that a heartfelt repentance could possibly postpone or even cancel God's impending judgement.

Convicted with courage and faith, Jeremiah spoke God's message of doom. His love compelled him to beg Judah to repent and weep in prayer for their forgiveness but Judah will not listen. Eventually, the Kingdom of Judah was conquered and destroyed by the Babylonians in 586 BC.

The conquest of Judah happened in two stages during the time King Josiah was making reforms to avert the bad policies of his grandfather King Manasseh between 641-609 BC, Babylon destroyed Assyria, and Egypt briefly imposed vassal status on Judah. Babylon defeated Egypt later and made Judah a Babylonian vassal in 605 BC. Judah revolted but was subjugated by Babylon in 597 BC. But Judah revolted again in 586 BC.. This revolt was the final one. Babylon destroyed Jerusalem and it's Temple and exiled it's King and many leading citizens in 586 BC ending the Judah's existence and inaugurating the Babylonia exile.

Even after Judah's destruction and exile, Jeremiah continued to love his people and warned them to submit to their oppressors and not rebel. Jeremiah informed them of God's promise to redeem a remnant of his people. God would make a new covenant with his people. This new would be written in their minds and on their hearts. God would be their God and they would be his people. God would show eternal grace, forgive their wickedness, and forget their sins forever (Jeremiah 31:33-34).

    We shall now turn our attention to the next book – Lamentations.

CHAPTER 26

Lamentations:
God Hears Our Cry.

The Book of Lamentations is a short book of a cry of grief and despair over the destruction of Jerusalem and it's Temple. It expresses the humiliation, suffering, and despair of Jerusalem and her people following the destruction of the city by the Babylonians in 586 BC.

When the Babylonians attacked Jerusalem, they destroyed the city and the Temple and exiled many of the dwellers of the city. Although the people had been warned many times by many Prophets, they could not believe that God would allow the destruction of the Temple. However, their sins caused the destruction.

The book contains five separate poems in five chapters. In chapter 1, the city sits as a desolate weeping widow overcome with miseries. In chapter 2, these miseries are described in connection with national sins and acts of God. Chapter 3 speaks of hope for the people of God and that the chastisement would only be for their good and a better day will dawn on them.

Chapter 4 laments the ruin and desolation of the city and the Temple, but traces it to the sins of the people. Chapter 5 is a prayer that Zion's reproach may be taken away in the repentance and recovery of the people.

In short, the book allows the people to offer a cry of repentance and sorrow over national sins and to pray for forgiveness and restoration.

The author of the book is anonymous. However, Lamentations has traditionally been ascribed to Jeremiah. This ascription of authorship to Jeremiah derives from the impetus to ascribe all Biblical books to inspired Biblical writers, and Jeremiah being a prophet at the time who prophesized it's destruction, was the obvious choice. But most modern scholars agree that Jeremiah did not write Lamentations; and so like most ancient Hebrew literature, the author remains anonymous.

The Babylonian's destruction of Jerusalem and the exile of many of it's dwellers caused an emotional and spiritual trauma. The people accept the reasons for the horrific punishment and express deep regret, sorrow, pain and repentance. Their lament remembers that God is compassionate and good, so their hope is in God's mercy and salvation.

C H A P T E R 2 7

Ezekiel: Is God Present With Us?

The Book of Ezekiel deals with one of the most important questions for God's people: Is God present with us or has he abandoned us?. The book bears the name of Ezekiel Ben Buzi who was born into a priestly family of Jerusalem around 623 BC, during the reign of the reforming King Josiah. Prior to this time, Judah had been a vassal state of the Assyrian Empire but the rapid decline of Assyria after 630 BC, led Josiah to assert his independence and institute a religious reform stressing loyalty to Yahweh, the national God of Israel.

Josiah was killed in 609 BC and Judah became a vassal of the new regional power the Neo- Babylonia Empire.

In 597 BC following the a rebellion against Babylon, Ezekiel was among the large group of Judeans taken into captivity by the Babylonians.

Why were the Judeans taken into captivity? Well, the people had become rebellious and disobedient. They took for granted God's blessings and presence, and they were disloyal to the God of their ancestors. Yet for many years, and through many prophets, God warned them and called them back to himself.

At a point in 597 BC, God's Judgement arrived with terrible consequences. The Babylonian King Nebuchadnezzar conquered

Jerusalem and carried away many of the leaders of the nation— among them King Jehoachin, other government officials and priests. This was the first deportation. That group of people even as they were marched to Babylon some 800 miles away, continued to think that God would destroy the Babylonians soon and make thing right. To them, a self-deluded people, God sent the Prophet Ezekiel.

Through out his long ministry, in many creative ways, Ezekiel explained to the Israelites the meaning of God's presence with them. When God's people are faithful and humbly walk before God, God's presence is a source of blessings, peace, and fruitfulness. However, when God's people are disloyal, rebellious and adulterous, God's presence is a terrifying thing because it means judgement and correction. However because God is merciful and compassionate, his presence also means forgiveness, salvation, restoration and hope.

The Book is divided into four major chapters:

1. Introduction and Call of Ezekiel (1-3).
2. The Coming Destruction and Captivity of Israel (4+24).
3. The Judgement against other Nations (25-32).
4. The Restoration of God's people (33-48).

In the inaugural vision of Ezekiel in Chapters 1-3:27, God approached Ezekiel as a divine warrior, riding in His battle chariot. The chariot is drawn by four living creatures, each having four faces –11 those of a man, a lion, an ox, and an eagle and four wings. Beside each "living creature" is a "wheel within a wheel", with " tall and awesome" rims full of eyes all around. God commissions Ezekiel as a prophet and as a "watchman" in Israel: " Son of man, I am sending you to the Israelites": (2:3).

In chapters 4:1–24:27, Judgement on Jerusalem and Judah and on other Nations is announced. God warns of the certain destruction of Jerusalem and the devastation of the nations that have troubled His people: the Ammonites, Moabites, and Philistines, the Phoenicean cities of Tyre and Sidon, and Egypt.

The building of a new city is recorded in Chapters 33:1–48:35). The Jewish exile will come to an end, a new city and a new Temple will be built, and Israel will be gathered and blessed as never before.

To Ezekiel, the destruction of Jerusalem was a purificatory sacrifice upon the altar made necessary by the " abomination" in the Temple — the presence of idols and the worship of the god Tammuz described in chapter 8.

In the conclusion of the book of Ezekiel, the Prophet announces that a small remnant will remain true to Yahweh in exile, will return to purify the city. The image of the valley of dry bones returning to life in chapter 37, signifies the restoration of the purified Israel.

The book reminds us not to become complacent by taking for granted God's grace and blessings like the Israelites did.

CHAPTER 28

Daniel: Living in Exile

Most of what we know about Daniel comes from the Book of Daniel. He was part of the first wave of exiled people from Jerusalem who were deported to Babylon in 605 BC. He was a member of the ruling religious class of Jerusalem, who were the first to be deported. Arriving in Babylon as a young man, Daniel and his friends were trained as court officials.

Because of God's blessings, he rose quickly and became "the third highest ruler in the Kingdom" (Daniel 5:29). He ministered from the first year of King Nebuchadnezzar in 605 BC to Cyrus's third year in 535 BC.

The book of Daniel has two sections and two purposes. The first part of the book tells about the life of Daniel and his friends in the Babylonian court (Chapters 1-6). The purpose of this section is to teach the exiled Israelites in Babylon how to live as God's people in a foreign, hostile land.

The second part of the book includes several visions and dreams that tell about future world events and how they affect God's people (Chapters 7-12). The purpose of this section is also to encourage God's people in time of suffering and persecution by assuring them that history is under God's control. God will do wonders that will dwarf anything he had done before.

Although the two sections are very different, they have a common theme: God rules over all. The book urges us to remember that if God has been faithful in history, then we can rest assured that he continues to be faithful and the future is victorious for God and his people.

A deeper study of the book reveals that first, God is an active God. Daniel reveals that God is not merely a passive "Lord of heavens" but he is the dynamic Lord of all and is closely involved in the lives of his people (Daniel 2:29-23).

Second, God is a Saving and Judging God who is a Ruler of the universe, the righteous judge of kings, nations, and history. He is also a powerful and compassionate savior of his people (Daniel 3:28-29, 7:13-14).

Third, God is Sovereign God. He rules over history. The future is no accident to God. He knows it and is intimately involved in working out his plans (Daniel 7:23-27, 8:9).

Fourth, God is breaking through in history. God will send his Man. The designation "Son of Man" as a title for the coming Messiah, is revealed in Daniel and this was Jesus' favorite term for himself (Daniel 7:13-14, 9:25-26).

Lastly, there is a hint of God and Resurrection. Though hinted in other books (Psalms, Job, Ezekiel), Daniel is the first to speak clearly about the hope of Resurrection (Daniel 12:1-2, 13).

Interestingly, Daniel is one of few books in the Old Testament that is written in two languages. Most of the Old Testament was written in Hebrew, the language of Israel. However, significant portions of Daniel (Daniel 2:4-7:28) are written in language known as the Imperial Aramaic. Because this was the language of much of the ancient Near East, the Babylonian Empire used it for official communication.

For many years, being God's people meant enjoying the Promised Land, worshipping God at the Temple, and learning and following the law. After the people were captured and exiled to Babylon, God preserved them. The question was how could they learn to be God's people, loyal and obeadient while living as a minority in a foreign land? How could they worship and honor God without the temple?.

The book of Daniel shows through the life of Daniel and his friends, and through the powerful prophecies about the future, what it meant to be God's people and how to be faithful to the God of our ancestors.

The life of Daniel and his friends remind us that God is with us, that his promises are reliable, and that he is in control because God is King. Moreover, although we still suffer in this world, we know that Daniel's vision about the future, ensures that justice will be vindicated, that evil be destroyed and that " at the mention of the name Jesus every knee should bow in heaven and on earth and under the earth, every tongue confess that Jesus Christ is Lord"

(Philippians 2:19-11).

C H A P T E R   2 9

Hosea: A Spiritually Bankrupt Nation.

Hosea was the son of Beeri and was an eighth century BC prophet. He was active between 750-722 BC as a prophet of Israel the Northern Kingdom with capital in Samaria. His book emphasizes the importance of the covenant and the results of breaking it. Hosea is a window into the heart of God. During his time of prophecy, Israel's desire to seek other gods and manuever politically is seen as spiritual adultery and breaks God's heart.

To illustrate this, Hosea's faithfulness towards his unfaithful wife is an example of God's commitment to his covenant and his beloved. The prophecy in the book anticipates God's judgement against Israel for breaking the covenant and calls the people to repent and renew their relationship with God.

At this point, let me explain what a covenant is. In a literal sense, a covenant is a binding agreement, a legal contract..It is sealed between two or more parties. In the Bible, covenant is a dominant theme in the Scriptures and serves as a foundation to the story of God's people. In a Biblical sense, the word covenant is derived from the same root word meaning " to cut". This means that in the culture of the Bible, covenant carries weight and was often cut or sealed in blood.

There are major Biblical Covenants in the Bible. One familiar to the Scriptures is one that God made with Abraham in Genesis Chapters 15-17. In this covenant, God gave a promise to Abraham that he would be the father of many nations. It happened at a time when he and his wife Sarah were barren. The sign was in the cutting of the flesh in circumcision.

Another significant covenant in the Bible is called the Mosaic covenant — it is the one God made with Israel. The Lord told Moses in Exodus Chapter 19 that if Israel will uphold the conditions to faithfully listen and obey,

God would uphold His end of the covenant. This means the Israelites were to become guardians of God's covenant. That means living out the commandments as a light to the nations. This was the basis for the calling of Israel to be a priest for the nations of the earth. So God called Israel in the midst of people or groups that walked in darkness– the people who did not live according to the law. It is this covenant that the people of Israel did not keep that engendered the prophecy of Hosea.

There were other covenants: the covenant that God made with King David to establish his throne forever. Then there is a New Covenant spoken of in Jeremiah Chapter 31 with the house of Israel where God's law would be written on the hearts of his people: " I will be their God and they shall be my people" (Jeremiah 31:33).

So the problem in Israel during Hosea time was that the people were not keeping the Covenant. The practice of idolatry, injustice, unrighteousness, rebellion, distain, arrogance and very scandalous behavior of God's people was sickening. The prophecy of Hosea as a result of this, calls the people of Israel to repent and renew their relationship with God. To worsen the situation, after many decades of peace and prosperity for Israel, Assyria began to emerge as a powerful empire in 800 BC. It started expanding westward and imposed their power on Israel and Israel's neighbors by forcing them to submit and pay tribute.

In 743 BC, King Tiglath Pileser III of Assyria put into effect a policy of deporting conquered people from their native land and bring other exiles from other nations to take their place. This policy was to prevent rebellion from the conquered people. Instead of Israel keeping their covenant with God for protection, Israel tried to form many alliances with Assyria, the neighboring nations and Egypt. These alliances expressed their lack of trust in God and led them to idolatry, the subject of Hosea's prophecy.

The message of Hosea is outlined as follows:

> ** Hosea and his unfaithful wife
> (Chapters 1-3).
> ** The Judgement of Israel (9-10).
> ** God expresses his love for Israel
> (11:1-11).
> **. God expresses his anger against Israel
> (11:12- 13:16).
> **. The Restoration of Israel (Chapter 14).

It must be stressed again that Hosea's prophecy was primarily addressed to the audience of the Northern Kingdom of Israel with Ephraim as a central and influencial tribe. There are many themes in his prophecy. His prophecy emphasizes that disobedience separates us from God. Only repentance and confession can bring restoration. Also, God judges and punishes disobedience. The people of Israel would not be spared for breaking the covenant.

Our major take away is that in all our sinfulness, God calls us to repentance because he is faithful and his love is everlasting and he promises redemption and restoration. In view of this, God will never give up on us, and he will always be faithful to his promises to always be our God and to provide for us. As seen in the case of the Israelites, despite their unfaithfulness, God promised to keep a remnant safe. Through that remnant, God sent His Son, the Messiah Jesus Christ.

CHAPTER 30

Joel: The Dreadful Day of the Lord.

Joel is the second prophet of the twelve Minor Prophets and the author of the Book of Joel. The book calls the people of Judah to repentance and warns them and their neighbors of a future time when God will judge them. He speaks of " the Day of the Lord" explaining that in that day, God will pour out his Spirit on the nations. The day is also a day of judgement against God's enemies.. Joel assures Judah's future safety from these threats, and promises full redemption.

By the time he was called to minister to Judah, the Southern Kingdom had been in a state of disarray and decline for many years, both economically and spiritually. Rival nations and city states such as Tyre, Sidon, and Philitia had made frequent incursions into Israel and a recent locust plaque and drought had devasted Judah's economy.

Like many Biblical Prophets, Joel was sent by God to get the people's attention in a time of depression and decline. However, unlike many prophets, Joel does not address specific sin or idolatry on the part of Judah. Rather, he uses the recent calamity of the locust to teach a prophetic lesson.

Throughout the book, the theme of disaster is prevalent. Looking back at the economic hardship brought on by the locust plaque was intended to encourage the people to look forward to a great and terrible day of the Lord– a day when the Sovereign God would judge the people and the nations who had rebelled against Him. Joel shares how God often uses nature and events like famine, plaque, violent weather, invading armies and celestial phenomena to get our attention (Joel 1:5).

Nevertheless, Joel prophesies that judgement can be averted if people repent, fast and return to the Lord and " rend your hearts and not your garments" (Joel 2:13-17).

But we know from history that Joel's warning went unheeded. As a result, "the Day of the Lord" in Scripture was partially fulfilled through the Babylonian conquest and invasion. However, deliverance is promised as well as restoration. Furthermore, Joel prophesies the outpouring of the Holy Spirit (Joel 2:28-29).

The prophecies of Joel reminds us that in uncertain times when God's people are threatened and surrounded by their enemies, God promises to bring solution to his people and empower them by pouring the Holy Spirit upon all believers to allow us to be adopted into God's kingdom and to empower us to be God's holy people, nation and royal priesthood (2 Peter 2:9).

C H A P T E R   3 1

Amos: Nation in Disarray

The Book of Amos is the third of the Minor Prophets. Amos who is the author, was a native of Tekoa— a town 12 miles from Jerusalem. He flourishes during the reigns of King Uzzah (783-742 BC) of Judah the Southern Kingdom and Jeroboam II (786-746 BC) of Israel the Northern Kingdom.

By occupation, Amos was a shepherd: whether he was merely that or a man of some means, no one knows. But surely he preached only for a short time.

Under the impact of powerful visions and divine destruction of the Hebrews in such natural disasters as a swarm of locusts, Amos travelled from Judah to the neighboring and more powerful Kingdom of Israel to preach.

He fiercely castigated corruption and social injustice among Israel's neighbors, Israel itself, and Judah.

What was happening at this time during the reign of Jeroboam Ii was that the Kingdom of Israel was enjoying a prosperous period. They were wealthy with a significant military and political power in the region. As a result, many individuals in the Kingdom especially high-ranking officials were living luxuriously, indulging in idol worship and immoral behavior, and mistreating the poor. As prosperity increased in Israel, so did immorality and injustice. The nation believed that because they were prosperous, they were within God's grace. God sent Amos to correct this misinterpretation.

Amos brought words about imminent judgement upon Israel because the people of Israel corrupted the worship of God, treated the poor and the weak with injustice and betrayed their covenant vows with God. The result of their disobedience and lack of mercy would be their destruction at the hands of a foreign nation.

Nevertheless, he stressed that God is merciful. Judgement is never God's last word. Amos provided them with a glimpse of hope. God would preserve a remnant in Israel who would return to the Promised Land and would remain in Israel forever (Amos 9:15).

After preaching at Bethel, a famous shrine under special protection of Jeroboam Ii, Amos was ordered to leave Israel under Jeroboam' priest Amazia and nothing is heard about Amos anymore.

God's call to Israel in Amos' time is just as relevant to us today. The Prophet challenged people to worship with their hearts and to be compassionate to those in weak social structures. And so as God's people,we are called to seek justice and care for the poor.

The two major themes in the book that we need to highlight are Social Justice and Proper Worship.

The consistent message of the Scriptures is that God's people ought to care for the poor, the widow, and the weak (Exodus 22:22-27, Deuteronomy 23:19, 24:6-27; Amos 2:6-7, 5:12-12). The Old Testament Prophets treated social injustice as seriously as idolatry, Amos shows this in his prophecy (Amos 2:6-7, 5:11-12, 8:4-6).

Concerning proper worship, God does not desire meaningless ritual and heartless performance of religious rites. God does desire mercy, justice, righteousness, obedience and heartfelt worship.

Today Jesus commands us to feed the hungry, to cloth the naked, to welcome the outcast, to care for the sick, and to visit the imprisoned (Matthew 25:31-46). And just as he critized the religious leaders for offering " lip service" to God, but not truly living a fruitful and God-pleasing life, we must be careful not to fall into the same trap of worshipping God with our lips but our hearts are far away.

Obadiah: Judgement on the People of Edom

The Book of Obadiah is based on a prophetic vision concerning the fall of Edom, a mountain-dwelling nation whose founding father is Esau.

The author of the book is Obadiah. He was a prophet who lived in the Assyria Period. In the book, Obadiah describes an encounter with God, addresses Edom's arrogance and charges them for their "violence against your brother Jacob" (Obadiah 1:10).

Throughout most of the history of Judah, Edom was controlled absolutely from Jerusalem as a vassal state. Obadiah said the high elevation of their dwelling place in the mountains of Seir had gone to their head, and they had puffed themselves up in pride. "Though you soar like the eagle and make your nest among the stars, from there I will bring you down; declares the Lord" (Obadiah 1:4).

In the Siege of Jerusalem in 597 BC, Nebuchadnezzar II sacked Jerusalem and carried away the King of Judah, then installed a puppet ruler. The problem was that the Edomites helped the Babylonians loot the city. The writing of Obadiah in 570 BC suggests that the Edomites should have helped their brothers in Judah. So God says "On that day you stood aloof while strangers carried off his wealth and foreigners entered her gates and cast lots for Jerusalem, you were like one of them…. You marched through the gates of my people in their day of their disaster, nor gloat over them in their calamity in the day of their disaster, nor seize their wealth in the day of their disaster" (Obadiah 1:11, 13).

Obadiah said in judgement, God would wipe out the house of Esau forever, and not even a remnant would remain (Obadiah 1:18). The Edomites land would be possessed by Egypt and they would cease to exist as a people (Obadiah 1:15). The "Day of the Lord" was at hand for all nations,and someday, the children of Israel would return from their exile and possess the land of Edom (Obadiah 1:17-21).

The book is the shortest book of the Old Testament. It has only one chapter with twenty-one verses. The outline is simple:

1. God's judgement of Edom (1-9).
2. Edom's violations (19-14).
3. Israel's Victory (15-21).

Who were the Edomites you may ask? They had a Kingdom called Edom. It was a small Kingdom Southwest of the Dead Sea and South of Moab. The name of the kingdom was derived from Esau, whose name was Edom as recorded in Genesis 25:30. And so they were Esau's descendants and although related to the Israelites, they were often hostile to the Israelites. From the time of the Exodus, the Edomites refused to allow the Israelites to pass through their territory (Numbers 29:14-21).

Later, they made alliance against Israel and Judah (2 Kings16:6). In time, the Babylonians conquered and destroyed the Edomite Kingdom (Jeremiah 3, 6).

In Obadiah's prophecies, he promised the people of Judah that God will keep the promise he made to Abraham. His people will receive redemption and their promised inheritance. Today, Jesus has fulfilled the promises made to Abraham. And those who believe in Jesus receive redemption and their promised inheritance (Colossians 1:9-14).

CHAPTER 33

Jonah: The Merciful God

The Book of Jonah is one of the twelve Minor Prophets which tells of a Hebrew Prophet named Jonah, son of Amittal, who God calls and sent by God to prophesy the destruction of Nineveh but tries to escape this divine mission.

Unlike the other Minor Prophets, the Book is almost entirely narrative except a poem in Chapter 2. The actual prophetic word against Nineveh is given only in passing through the narrative.

In the book, Jonah is the central character in which God commands to go to the city of Nineveh to prophesy against it for their great wickedness against him (Jonah 1:2).

However, Jonah instead, attempts to run from God by going to Joppa and sailing to Tarshish. A huge storm arises and the sailors, realizing that it is no ordinary storm, cast lots and discover Jonah is to blame (Jonah 2:4-7). Jonah admits this and states if he is cast overboard, the storm will cease. The sailors refused to do this, but all their efforts fail and they are eventually forced to throw him overboard. As a result, the storm calms and the sailors then offer sacrifices to God.

Miraculously, Jonah is saved by being swallowed by a large fish, in whose belly he spends three days and three nights. While in the Great fish, Jonah prays to God in his suffering and commits to thanksgiving and vowing to obey God's instruction. God then commands the fish to vomit Jonah out (Jonah 2:10).

God once again commands Jonah to travel to Nineveh and prophesy to it's inhabitants. He goes into the city crying "In forty days Nineveh shall be overthrown" (Jonah 3:2-4). After he walked across Nineveh, the people begin to believe his word and proclaimed a fast. The King of Nineveh then puts on sackcloth and sits in ashes, making a proclamation which decrees fasting, the wearing of sackcloth, prayer and repentance. God sees their repentant hearts and spares the city at that time (Jonah 3:10).

Jonah was disappointed by this and refers to his earlier flight to Tarshish while asserting that since God is merciful it was inevitable that God would turn from the threatened calamities (Jonah 4:1-4). He then leaves the city and makes himself a shelter, waiting to see whether or not the city will be destroyed. A plant springs up overnight providing him welcome shelter from the heat but it is destroyed by a great worm. Jonah becomes bitter at the destruction of the plant but God speaks and thrusts home the final point of the story. "You pity the plant for which you did not labor, nor did you make it grow, which came into being in a night and perished in a night. And should I not pity Nineveh, that great city in which there are more than a hundred and twenty thousand persons who do not know their right hand from their left, and also much cattle?".

(Jonah Chapter 4: 10-11).

The lesson in the Book of Jonah is that God loves all people, everywhere and shows His love to all. It is not exclusive, it is universal and timeless. God will show compassion and mercy to anyone who repents and asks for forgiveness.

The story also challenges us to love our enemies and pray for those who persecute us. Nineveh was the capital city of the nation that threatened to destroy Israel and Jonah tried to run away. He did not want to preach repentance to his enemy. He wanted God to judge them harshly and not forgive them. Lastly, the story teaches us that no one can run away from God. Jonah tried to run from God but he couldn't.

CHAPTER 34

Micah: Love Mercy, Walk Humbly Seek Justice.

The Book of Micah was authored by Micah who was from a town of Moresheth located Southwest of Jerusalem. He began his prophetic career during the reign of King Jothan (750-732 BC), through the reign of King Ahaz (734-716 BC), and completed his prophecies during the reign of Hezekiah (716- 687 BC).

During the time of his prophecies, Israel, Judah and the other nations of the region came under increasing pressure from the aggressive and rapidly expanding Assyria Empire after a long period of peace.

Between 734 and 627 BC, Tiglath Pileser II of Assyria conducted almost annual campaigns in Palestine, reducing the Kingdom of Israel, the Kingdom of Judah and the Philistine cities to vassalage, receiving tribute from Ammon, Moab and Edom, and absorbing Damascus (the Kingdom of Aram) into the Empire.

On Tiglath Pileser death, Israel rebelled, resulting in Assyrian counter attack and the destruction of the capital, Samaria, in 722 BC after a three- year siege. Micah in Chapter 2:2-7 draws on this event and says Samaria has been destroyed by God because of it's crimes of idolatry, oppression of the poor, and misuse of power.

In the Book of Micah, the prophet prophesied against the leadership of this people for their injustice, greed, and lack of humility. He brought words about God's justice, the destruction of Samaria the capital of Israel, and the fall of Jerusalem the capital of Judah.

However, he also proclaimed a vision of redemption and forgiveness. Micah promised that a remnant would return, regain their inheritance and worship the Lord. He explains that true worship means " to act justly and to love mercy and to walk humbly with your God"(Micah 6:8).

In all his prophecies, he stressed that God judges and punishes disobedience, God is loving and faithful to his promises, God hates injustice, idolatry, greed, lack of mercy, and empty ritualistic religion, and God desires mercy, humility and justice.

Above all, Micah prophesized the birthplace of Jesus in Bethlehem, but more than that this prophecy states that this " shepherd" will lead God's people into an eternal kingdom that will reach to the ends of the earth(Micah 5:2-5).

The greatest lesson to learn from the Book of Micah is that true worship means to seek justice, love mercy, and to walk humbly with God.

CHAPTER 35

Nahum: The Destruction of Assyria's Capital—Nineveh

The Prophet Nahum, from the town of Elkosh, lived at the time of Zephaniah and the young Jeremiah. The book describes the prophet's vision of events leading up to the fall of Nineveh the Capital city of the Assyrian Empire in 612 BC. Although the book deals with the future of the Assyrian capital, Nineveh, Nahum's prophecy was primarily for the people of Judah.

Ashurbanipal who was King of Assyrian Empire from 669 BC to his death in 631 BC, was at the height of his glory. Nineveh was a city of vast extent, and was then the center of the civilization and commerce of the world. According to Nahum, it was a "bloody city full of lies and robbery" (Nahum 3:1), a reference to the Assyrian Empire's military campaigns and demand of tribute and plunder from conquered cities.

Remember that Jonah had already uttered his message of warning, and Nahum was followed by Zephaniah, who predicted the destruction of the city (Zephaniah 2:4-25).

Well, Nineveh was destroyed in 625 BC, and the Assyrian Empire came to an end– an event that changed the face of Asia. The Babylonian Chronicle of the fall of Nineveh tells the story of the end of Nineveh. Nebopolasser who was the founder and first King of the Babylonian

Empire from 626:BC to 695 BC joined forces with Cyaxares, King of the Medes, and laid siege for three months and conquered the city of Nineveh.

The Prophet Jonah shows where God shows concern for the people of Nineveh while Nahum's writings testifies to his belief in righteousness and justice of God, and how God dealt with those Assyrians in punishment according to their cruelty.

From it's opening, Nahum shows God to be slow to anger, but God will by no means ignore the guilty. God will bring his vengeance and wrath to pass. God is presented as a God who will punish evil, but will protect those who trust in Him (Nahum 1:2-3).

Therefore, God's judgement on Nineveh is " all because of the wonton lust of a harlot, alluring, the mistress of the sorceries, who enslaved nations hy her prostitution and people by her witchcraft" (Nahum 3:4). Infidelity according to the Prophets, is related to spiritual unfaithfulness: " the land is guilty of the vilest adultery in departing from God"(Hosea 1:2).;

The Book of Nahum teaches us that when we are kind and merciful, God will show us kindness and mercy. But when we are heartless, God will judge us sternly. Nineveh was punished for being heartless and wicked just as Nahum prophesied.

CHAPTER 36

Habakkuk: Why Does Evil Go Unpunished?

In the Book of Habakkuk, the Prophet wrestles with the question: "Why does God allow people to get away with evil?". Habakkuk wonders why God tolerates wickedness amongst his people.

After God answers him, the Prophet is perplexed by how God allows a wicked nation like the Babylonians to impart justice upon God's own people.

Let us deal with the background to Habakkuk's query. After the death of King Josiah the King of Judah in 609 BC, his son Jehoahaz was made King. After three months, Pharaoh Necho II deported Jehoahaz to Egypt and placed his brother Jehoiakim on the throne as a vassal to Egypt. Jehoiakim was a wicked king and evil flourished in Judah under his leadership.

Two decades after the death of King Josiah, the Babylonian Empire rose as a world power conquering one nation after another as they swept westward from Mesopotamia. In 586 BC, the Babylonians destroyed Judah and the Temple, and exiled most of Judah's inhabitants. So the theme of the Book of Habakkuk is trying to grow from a faith of perplexity and doubt to the height of absolute trust in God. Habakkuk addresses his concerns over the fact that God will use the Babylonian Empire to execute judgement on Judah for their sins.

He openly questions the wisdom of God.

In the first part of the first chapter, the Prophet sees the injustice amongst his people and asks why God does not take action, " Yahweh, how long will I cry, and you will not hear? I cry out to you" violence" and you will not save?" (Habakkuk 1:2).

In the middle part of chapter one, God explains that he will send the Chaldeans also known as the Babylonians to punish his people. "Look among the nations, watch, and wonder marvelously; for I am working a work in your days, which you will not believe though it is told you"

(Habakkuk 1:5). "For behold, I raised up the Chaldeans, that bitter and hasty nation, that marched through the breath of the nation, that marched through the breath of the earth, to possess dwelling places that are not theirs" (Habakkuk 1:6).

In the final part, of the first chapter, the prophet expresses shock at God's choice of the instrument for judgment. In chapter 1:13, the prophet asks: "You who have pure eyes than see evil, and who cannot look on perversity, why do you tolerate those who deal treacherously, and keep silent when the wicked swallows up the man who is more righteous than he?".

In chapter two, he awaits God's answer to his challenge. God answers his challenge. God explains .that He will also judge the Chaldeans, and much more harshly "because you have plundered many nations, all the remnant of the peoples will plunder you, because of men's blood, and for the violence done to the land, to the city and to all who dwell in it. Woe to him who gets an evil gain of his house" (Habakkuk 2:8-9).

Finally in chapter three, Habakkuk expresses his ultimate faith in God, even if he does not fully understand. " For though the fig tree does not flourish, nor fruit be in vines, the labor of the olive fails, the field yields no food, the flocks are cut off from the fold, and there is no herd in the stalls; yet I will rejoice in Yahweh. I will be joyful in the God of my salvation" (Habakkuk 3:17-18).

The theme of the book is clear: God's justice is mysterious, why does it seem that God tolerates evil?, and God is powerful and in control.

What we learn from the Book of Habakkuk is that God will bring justice, but his timing is not the same as ours. God's answer to Habakkuk can provide insight into our difficult questions. Sometimes, it appears that God tolerates evil by allowing the wicked to prosper and the good to suffer. Habakkuk addresses these issues and challenges us to trust in God and live in faithful obedience to him.

C H A P T E R   3 7

Zephaniah: Repent or Perish

The Prophet Zephaniah is identified as the son of Cushi, the son of Gedaliah, the son of Mariah, the son of Hezekiah (1:1).

Zephaniah ministered during the reign of King Josiah (642-609 BC). The book was intended for the people of Judah as a warning of God's coming judgement for it's refusal to obey it's covenant obligations toward Yahweh despite having seen Israel exiled a generation or two previously— an exile that the Judahite literaly tradition attributed to Yahweh's anger against Israel's disobedience to his covenant.

In this historical context, Zephaniah urges Judah to be obedient to Yahweh, saying that perhaps he will forgive them if they do (Zeph. 2:3).

The problem was that in Judah, King Josiah was the good king of Judah. He put in place several reforms in Judah from 632 BC to 621BC. He reigned during a political and military transition in the world around Judah. After the death of Assyrian ruler Ashurbanipal in 627 BC, the Assyrian Empire began to decline rapidly. For that reason, the Babylonian Empire began to increase in power and influence, overcoming Assyria and destroying the Assyrian capital Nineveh in 612 BC.

Although Josiah was the last King of Judah's good kings, Israel and Judah's sins in the past, especially those of Manasseh (2 Kings 21:1-18), led the kingdom away from God. God delayed his just punishment of

Judah because of Josiah's reforms. However, Zephaniah reminded them that God's punishment would come and it will be terrible.

His theme was "the Day of the Lord". God will judge the nations and destroy them. God calls us to repentance and God will restore a remnant of his people and keep his promises.

Indeed, God kept his promises and restored a remnant of his people. Out of that remnant, God sent his only Son to redeem his people for eternity, saving us from complete destruction on the day of thebLord. One day, God will judge and destroy those who live in sin and continue in their wickedness. The Book of Zephaniah challenges us to avoid our sinful ways, repent and seek God's redemption found in Jesus Christ.

CHAPTER 38

Haggai: Think Careful About Your Ways.

The Book of Haggai records events in 520 BC; 18 years after Cyrus had conquered Babylon and issued a decree in 538 BC, allowing the captive Judahite to return to Judea. Cyrus saw the restoration of the temple as necessary for the restoration of religious practices, and a sense of peoplehood after the exile.

In Haggai's day, the Jews had returned to Jerusalem after 70 years of exile to foreign land. At first, they enthusiastically began rebuilding God's temple but then fell into apathy and stopped construction (Haggai 1:2). God's message through Haggai challenged the people to wake up from their spiritual slumber and take on the task at hand because God Almighty is with them and will bless them when they make him their first priority.

Why did they fall into apathy and stopped the construction? Well, the economy of this region was slow. The people worked hard, but could never seem to prosper as they had expected (Haggai 1:5-6, 9). Perhaps this was the reason why they said "the time has not yet come for the Lord's house to be built" (1:2). They were waiting for a time of prosperity before they would turn their attention to spiritual matters. So in a time of widespread indifference toward serving the Lord, the

Prophet Haggai challenged God's people to "give careful thoughts to your ways" (1:5).

To Haggai, the temple was a sign of God's presence with his people. To neglect building the Temple demonstrated great apathy towards God. The people lived in their paneled houses, but the Lord's house remained in ruins (1: 4,9). Once the people responded to Haggai's message, and resumed rebuilding the temple, God promised to fill his temple with glory and bless his people (2:9, 19).

Haggai reports that three weeks after his first prophecy, the rebuilding of the temple began in September 7, 521 BC "they came and began work on the house of the Lord Almighty their God, on the twenty- fourth day of the sixth month in the second year of Darius the King" (Haggai 1:14-15)

The Book of Ezra indicates that it was finished on February 25, 516 BC. "The temple was completed on the third day of the month Adar, in the sixth year of the reign of King Darius (Ezra 6:15).

For Haggai, the fact that the ground produced little and that resources were scarce was not simply a matter of needing better farming methods or better planning. It was primarily a spiritual matter. The people needed God's blessings. They needed to take up the spiritual work God had called them to instead of just their own work.

Haggai's message rings just as true for us today. No matter what our financial situation may be, we must make God our first priority. When we do, God assures us that he will be with us and bless us. "And my God will supply all your needs according to the riches of his glory in Christ Jesus" (Philippians 4:19).

CHAPTER 39

Zechariah: The Lord
Rules Over All

The Book of Zechariah is attributed to the Prophet Zechariah. He was a prophet of priestly lineage, born in Babylon and came to Jerusalem with the exiled who returned under Zerubbabbel (Zech.1:1,7; Neh. 12:4,16). He is mentioned along with the older prophet Haggai in Ezra 5:1 and 6:14.

The purpose of the book is not strictly historical but theological and pastoral. The main emphasis of Zachariah's prophecies is that God is at work and all his good deeds, including the construction of the Second Temple, are accomplished "not by might or power, but by my Spirit" (Zech. 4:6). Ultimately, God plans to live again with His people in Jerusalem. He will save them from their enemies and cleanse them from sin. However, God requires repentance, a turning away from sin towards faith in Him.

Zechariah's prophecies took place during the reign of Darius the Great (Zech:1:1). He was contemporary with Haggai in the post- exilic world after the fall of Jerusalem in 586 BC. During the exile, many Judahites and Benjamites were taken to Babylon where the prophets told them to make their homes, suggesting they would spend a long time there.

Eventually, freedom did come to many Israelites when Cyrus the Great overtook the Babylonians in 539 BC. The famous Edict of Cyrus was released in 538 BC and the first return took place under Sheshbazzar. After the death of Cyrus in 530 BC, Darius consolidated power and took office in 522 BC.

His system divided the different colonies of the empire into easily manageable districts overseen by governors. This is where Zerubbabbel comes into the picture. He was appointed by Darius as governor over the district of Yehud Medinata in the southwest part of Judah.

It was under the rule of Darius that the Prophet Zechariah emerged, centering on the rebuilding of the Temple. Zechariah reminds the people that God is Sovereign and faithful to his covenant with them. He is on their side. Along with the Prophet Haggai, Zechariah encouraged the people who returned to Jerusalem after many years in exile to continue rebuilding the temple.

The Book of Zechariah not only looks at the present situation in which the people are reestablishing their Homeland and building the temple, but it also looks towards a day when God's Sovereignty will be recognized throughout the world and all people will come to worship the Lord (Zech. 2:11; 6:15:14:6).

Zechariah not only encouraged God's people to build the physical temple, but also reminded them that they were really building a future kingdom far beyond the borders of Jerusalem in which the Messiah will reign in power.

Believers today can see in the New Testament how Jesus fulfilled many of Zechariah's prophecies. As believers, we too wait for a coming day when we will see the fullness of Jesus' Kingdom over all the earth.

C H A P T E R   4 0

Malachi: The Day of the Lord

The Book of Malachi is the last book in the Old Testament and also the last of the Minor Prophets. Nothing personal is known about the Prophet Malachi whose name simply means " my Messenger" (1:1).

Thebook was written to correct the lax religious and social behavior of the Israelites– particularly the priests in post exilic Jerusalem. Although the Prophets urged the people of Judah and Israel to see their exile as punishment for failing to uphold their Covenant with God, it was not long after they had been restored to the land and to Temple worship that the people's commitment to their God began once again to wane. It was in this context that the Prophet Malachi delivered his prophecy.

In Chapter 1:2, Malachi had the people of Israel question God's love for them. This introduction to the book illustrates the seriousness of the situation which he addresses. He confronts his audience and proceeds to accuse them of failing to respect God as God deserves. One way in which this disrespect is made clear is through the substandard sacrifices which he claims are being offered by the priests. While God demands animals that are "without blemish" (Lev. 1:3), the priests who were to determine whether the sacrifice was acceptable, were offering blind to lame, and sick animals for sacrifice because they thought nobody would notice.

– 104 –

In Chapter 2:1, Malachi warns that God is sending a curse on the priests who have not honored Him with appropriate animal sacrifices." Now, watch how I am going to paralyze your arm and throw dung in your face— dung from your very solemnities– and sweep you away with it. Then you shall learn that it is I who has given you this warning of my intention to abolish my covenant with Levi, says Yahweh Saboath".

In Chapter 2:10, he addresses the issue of divorce. On this, he deals with divorce both as a social problem and as a religious problem: " Judah has married the daughter of a foreign god" (Malachi 2:11). He also criticizes his audience for questioning God's justice. He reminds them that God is just and exhorts them to be faithful as they wait for justice. He quickly points out to the people that they have not been faithful. In fact, the people are not giving all that God deserves. Just as the priests have been offering unacceptable sacrifices, so the people have been neglecting to offer their full tithe to God. The result of these shortcomings is the people have come to believe that no good comes out serving God. He assures the faithful amongst his audience that in the end times, the difference between those who serve God faithfully and those who do not will become clear. Malachi concludes by calling upon the teachings of Moses and by promising that Elijah will return prior to the Day of the Lord.

It can be very tempting to doubt, like the people of Malachi s day, that it really makes a difference whether we serve and obey the Lord. But the Book of Malachi assures us that God will act, and when he does, he will do so in power and judgement. Things will be different on the Day of the Lord.

THE EPILOGUE

This concludes our Short Study of the Old Testament. I hope you have enjoyed our journey through the Old Testament, learnt something new and that you have been encouraged to take your time to read the books in the Old Testament. Thank you for coming along with me on this journey. God bless, keep and watch over you as you put your trust in the Living God. Shalom!

Printed in the United States
by Baker & Taylor Publisher Services